GET YOUR BAKE ON

GET YOUR BAKE ON

Sweet and Savory Recipes From My Home to Yours

Brian Emmett

Gallery Books

New York   London   Toronto   Sydney   New Delhi

G

Gallery Books
An Imprint of Simon & Schuster, Inc.
1230 Avenue of the Americas
New York, NY 10020

First Gallery Books trade paperback edition May 2015

GALLERY BOOKS and colophon are registered trademarks of Simon & Schuster, Inc.

For information about special discounts for bulk purchases, please contact
Simon & Schuster Special Sales at 1-866-506-1949 or business@simonandschuster.com.

The Simon & Schuster Speakers Bureau can bring authors to your live event.
For more information or to book an event, contact the Simon & Schuster Speakers Bureau
at 1-866-248-3049 or visit our website at www.simonspeakers.com.

Designed by Davina Mock-Maniscalco

Manufactured in the United States of America

10   9   8   7   6   5   4   3   2   1

Library of Congress Cataloging-in-Publication Data

Emmett, Brian, 1969–
  Get your bake on : sweet and savory recipes from my home to yours / Brian Emmett.
          pages cm
  1. Baking. 1. Title.
  TX763.E63 2015
  641.81'.5—dc23
                                   2014048393

ISBN 978-1-4767-7256-1
ISBN 978-1-4767-7259-2 (ebook)

Acknowledgments

I feel so blessed to be able to write my first cookbook; it has been a fantastic journey and I have so many people to thank.

First and foremost, the Lord above, who helps me every day and gives me the strength and courage to follow my dreams and never give up.

My beautiful and loving (and sometimes fiery) wife, Lisa, for believing in me and sacrificing so much for our family to allow me to follow my dreams and passions. You were by my side at each audition and we finally did it!

My daughters, Shayla and Julia, for making me a proud dad, challenging me, and being my ultimate taste-testers.

My best friend and business partner, Mike, for putting up with me and always encouraging me to move forward and never look back. Oh . . . and for being another one of my ultimate taste-testers.

To my beautiful mother, Nancy, who taught me how to be a kind, loving, and caring man. And . . . for teaching me how to bake and cook my butt off.

My grandmothers, Lillian and Marianne, may they rest in peace, on whose heels I followed into the kitchen, trying to find out what they were whipping up.

My mother-in-law, Dorothy, for inspiring me to try new things in the kitchen and sparking my love of European culture, including olive oil and vino!

My wife's grandmother, Mima, for introducing me to Cuban cuisine, teaching me patience in the kitchen, and making me laugh. "Ay, chico!" Miss you.

My food editor, Sarah Mastracco, for her guidance throughout the process of writing this book. Her food knowledge is amazing, and I couldn't have done it without her.

To my photography and food stylist team . . . you truly made this book come alive with beautiful food and photos that represent the spirit and essence of my cooking style as a baker and a chef. Thanks to: Mark Ferri (photographer), Leslie Orlandini (food stylist), Amanda Heckert (food stylist assistant), Francine Matalon-Degni (prop stylist), and Jamie Slater (photo assistant). What a memorable three days it was for me!

My good friend, Mia, the best fitness trainer in the world, for pushing me beyond limits in the gym and for being a true inspiration.

My many fans for following me on this journey and for loving all the food pictures I post daily. You are as much an inspiration to me as I am to you.

All the people at Simon and Schuster and Gallery Books who made this book possible; there are too many to name.

Love Productions and CBS for creating *The American Baking Competition*—the best cooking show on TV.

Last but not least, to all my extended family and friends that come to all my soirees and dig into the delicious food, you inspire me to keep creating deliciousness!

Contents

Pies and Tarts

Scones, Muffins, and Biscuits

Breads and Pizzas

Cookies, Bars, Biscotti, and Brownies

Cakes

Pastry and Pie Dough

Soufflés and Custards

Introduction

What an amazing journey I have had since winning *The American Baking Competition*! One of my favorite sayings is "You Will . . . When You Believe." As I sit down to write this introduction, I cannot help but be overwhelmed with emotion, gratitude, and pleasure. I feel quite fortunate to have had such an experience, but it didn't come easily. When I decided to challenge myself through competitive cooking, the first door did not open, nor the second, or even the third. I tried out for several other shows before auditioning for *The American Baking Competition*. I'll tell you that I had my doubts, and in fact, the day before the audition I decided not to compete. My past experiences discouraged me, and I wasn't ready to get the rejection stamp again. And then my wife stepped in and said, "You can do this! You absolutely are competing, so get in that kitchen and whip up your cheesecake!" The rest, as they say, is history.

I have spent the better part of this last year traveling around the country, doing cooking demonstrations, making TV appearances, and having the time of my life! Along the way, I have met so many amazing, inspiring people, and I feel like I have learned as much from them as they have, hopefully, learned from me.

During my travels, I have noticed that I'm frequently asked this question:

"What does it take to become a great baker?" Well, my answer is this: Because baking is both an art and a skill, you should be willing to make mistakes. Making mistakes is a part of the learning and creative process, and working through the setbacks will only help you succeed in the long run. Excellence evolves over time, so don't be afraid of failing. Practice, practice, practice techniques and try different methods until you find what works best and gives you the results you're striving for. Have fun and let the time you spend baking be the best part of your day. You deserve it!

I remember when I first got married and I really started to turn up the heat on my culinary skills and prowess. I was invited to a dinner party and the hosts requested that I bring a banana cream pie. Because it's one of my very favorite desserts, and one that I've made about a million times, I was thrilled! When I finished making the pie, I thought the consistency of the filling was a little strange, but I just told myself, "Oh, it just has to set." Right? Well, I was completely wrong. When we got to the party, I cut into the pie and as my knife sliced through something that was much closer to the consistency of soup, I realized it definitely was not set. Not only that, but the flavor? Well, let's just say it was not what I would call sweet. And then it hit me like a brick—I FORGOT THE SUGAR! WOW, talk about embarrassing! The moral of the story is that you live and you learn. Now, whenever I make that banana cream pie, guess what I bring out first? You, the sugar! So it goes to show that practice makes perfect, and it's all about having fun and learning in the kitchen—mistakes are simply a part of the process.

I'm the ultimate foodie and home entertainer—as a matter of fact, I've been called The Male Martha Stewart by almost everyone who knows me. I am very particular about working neatly and staying organized, and to the surprise of many, I clean my kitchen counter periodically with a vacuum! My wife appreciates my obsessions in the kitchen and wisely watches from afar as I get into the "cooking zone," as she calls it. Of course, family is my inspiration, so once I'm out of the "zone," all are invited to share in the fruits of my labor.

I have been baking, cooking, and designing festive and one-of-a-kind culinary experiences for my family and friends for more than twenty years. I am constantly striving to be innovative and create new and amazing meals and party themes. My complete obsession with food, and with baking in particular, started when I was young as I watched, listened, and learned from my mother and grandmothers. They were always in the kitchen creating the most delicious food, and I would be on their heels—first observing and eating, then getting in on the cooking action as I got older. In fact, in grade school I entered my first baking competition. The theme was "The First Thanksgiving Meal," and each student had to come up with a dish that reflected the food served at that first harvest gathering in the 1600s. Even at such a young age, I had a love for baking because of my mother and grandmothers and I was super eager to participate. I decided to make a pumpkin cake, and to my huge surprise, I won first place!

I continued to hone my baking and cooking skills over the years, really kicking it into gear after getting married and becoming a dad. It was with strong encouragement from my family and friends that I entered *The American Baking Competition*, but it was my skill, perseverance, and confidence that led me to fight through the harder moments and ultimately be named America's Best Amateur Baker! Living this life of cooking, traveling, and teaching others has been a dream of mine since I was a little boy, and I made that dream become a reality. Believing in myself and practicing my craft with passion have paid off, and I am so thankful for all that has come from this experience. I feel that if you possess the ability to believe in yourself, you can conquer your fears and make anything happen.

DURING THE PROCESS of writing this book, I had the opportunity to learn something pretty amazing about my family history that I didn't know before.

My great-grandma Mae Griffin owned a bakery in downtown Chicago in the late 1800s and early 1900s. When my grandpa Griffin was twelve, he started working in the bakery with his mom, initially delivering baked goods to the locals on his bicycle and eventually graduating to become a baker in his own right. I was astounded and thrilled to learn that I come from a long line of bakers, but it helps me make sense of this deep passion and dedication I have for the art.

Just like my ancestors, I find that the ultimate way to express appreciation for my family and friends is by offering them the best food made with love. Now I have the opportunity to share some of my favorite kitchen creations with a whole new audience. This book is a culmination of a lifelong passion for baking that started in my childhood and has now opened up a new path in my life. It is NEVER too late to follow your dreams. Live well. Love much. Smile often. Take risks. And cook and bake your #@% off!

A Few Words of Wisdom
Before You Start Baking . . .

*I*t is very important to read a recipe completely BEFORE you start baking, as some steps may require equipment that you need to dig up from the depths of your pantry. Also, there may be time requirements that you will want to prepare for, like if little Sally needs to be picked up from soccer 20 minutes into your apple pie's baking time, or you need to run to the dry cleaner's before they close for the weekend right when your cakes have gone into the oven. Be prepared and know what kind of time you have before you start—it will make a difference in your final product.

You will also want to get all of your ingredients ready to roll before you start cooking. This is known as *mise en place*, which is French for "put in its place." Preheat your oven to avoid delays and to ensure accuracy, as most doughs and batters will turn out much better if they bake at the right temperature.

As you are baking, be aware of sights and smells, and trust your instincts. In other words, "use the force." If something smells like it's burning, it probably is. If your yeast-and-water mixture isn't getting foamy, maybe the water was not warm enough to activate the yeast. Don't be afraid to start over if you make a mistake or if something seems wrong—it's the best way to learn and become the best baker you can be. Rome wasn't built in a day . . . and neither was America's Best Amateur Baker. I've certainly made my fair share of mistakes, but passion and dedication push me to try again and learn from the missteps. Trust me when I say, it's worth it!

BASIC BAKING TOOLS AND EQUIPMENT

There are a few basic tools that you should have on hand to get started with the recipes in this book. Of course you will not need all of the equipment in this list, but having at least a few of these on hand will make the process much easier.

- Baking pans, rimmed and rimless

- Dry measuring cups for ingredients such as sugar, flour, and cocoa powder

- Liquid measuring cups for ingredients such as milk, water, and syrups

- Measuring spoons

- Standing electric mixer with paddle, whisk, and dough hook attachments for cake batters, cookie dough, bread dough, whipping cream, etc.

- Hand mixer for mixing, beating, and whipping

- Food processor for chopping and combining

- Scale for weighing

- Offset spatula for frosting and spreading batters and doughs

- Rubber spatula for scraping, mixing, and folding

- Wooden spoon for stirring

- Whisk for sifting and whisking

- Sieve for sifting

- Parchment paper, aluminum foil, and plastic wrap

- Pie weights (dry beans or rice work as weights, too!)

- Mixing bowls in various sizes

- Wire racks for cooling

- Rolling pin

- Ruler

- Pastry brush

- Microplane or grater for grating citrus zests and nutmeg

MEASURING AND WEIGHING

In baking, accurate measuring and weighing of ingredients is extremely important and learning the basics will help you throughout your process. Here are a few tips:

- Measure dry ingredients in dry measure cups as opposed to liquid measure cups. Scoop ingredients such as sugar, or fluff and spoon ingredients such as flour or confectioners' sugar into your measuring cup, then use the flat side of a knife to level it off.

- Measure wet ingredients such as milk, water, citrus juices, and syrups in liquid measuring cups. Place the measuring cup on a flat, level surface and then pour in the ingredient, keeping a keen eye on the liquid level.

- For ingredients that should be measured by weight, use a scale. Simple as that!

DRY MEASURE

Cup	Tablespoon	Teaspoon
1C	16T	48t
¾C	12T	36t
⅔C	10T + 2t	32t
½C	8T	24t
⅓C	5T + 1t	16t
¼C	4T	12t
⅛C	2T	6t
1/16C	1T	3t

LIQUID MEASURE

Cups	FL Ounces	Tablespoons	ML
1C	8oz	16T	237mL
¾C	6oz	12T	177mL
⅔C	5.3oz	10T + 2t	158mL
½C	4oz	8T	113mL
⅓C	2.7oz	5T + 1t	79mL
¼C	2oz	4T	59mL
⅛C	1oz	2T	30mL
1/16C	.5oz	1T	15mL

WEIGHT

Ounces	Grams	Pounds
8oz	227g	.50lbs
7oz	198g	.44lbs
6oz	170g	.38lbs
5oz	142g	.31lbs
4oz	113g	.25lbs
3oz	85g	.19lbs
2oz	57g	.13lbs
1oz	28g	.06lbs
.5oz	14g	.03lbs

PREPARING PANS AND BAKING SHEETS

Prepare your pans so that your baked goods do not stick or burn. There are several ways you can do this.

Line your baking pans and baking sheets with parchment paper or a non-stick baking mat if you have one. Use butter, oil, or nonstick baking spray to coat the bottom and sides of the pan, then dust it with flour, sugar, or cocoa powder (depending on the recipe), shake it to evenly coat the bottom and sides, and tap out the excess. For cakes, grease the pan with butter, oil, or nonstick baking spray, then cut out a circle of parchment paper to fit the bottom of the cake pan (this will make it easier to release the cake from the pan). If using a parchment round, make sure you grease it and dust it with flour as well.

When making recipes such as macarons (pages 108, 111, and 113) and Orange-Almond Dacquoise (page 164) that require precise measurements, trace the desired shape onto parchment paper with a pencil, flip the paper, then follow the outlines when piping or filling with batter.

INGREDIENTS

I'm often asked about baking ingredients and whether they should be cold or at room temperature. Almost all ingredients that you are going to bake with should be room temperature. The only time you will not use an ingredient at room temperature is when making things such as piecrust, puff pastry, and croissants. For these recipes the butter should be cold to ensure even distribution throughout the dough. Ingredients will be listed as "cold" in these instances.

It's important to always use the highest quality ingredients available. Here are some tips to keep in mind when shopping:

- **EGGS:** I like to use large brown organic eggs because the yolk is richer and stands up better to the baking process. Make sure you look at expiration dates as expired eggs could cause issues with taste and health.

- **BUTTER:** Butter should be unsalted unless otherwise noted, and look for a butter that has a higher fat content (sometimes labeled "European style"), which will give you the best taste. The difference is that standard grocery store butter has around 81% fat content, while European-style butter has about 83% or higher.

- **SUGARS:** Use granulated sugar unless otherwise noted, as it blends well and dissolves fast. If you would like to try other sugars, such as raw or turbinado sugar, in place of granulated, do your research first—it may impact the flavor and consistency of your baked goods.

- **FLOUR:** There are many varieties of flour. Most of the recipes in this book call for all-purpose unbleached flour. If you want to substitute, again, do your research first. Flour can also become stale, which will affect the quality of your baked goods, so make sure you use the freshest flour available.

- **FRESH FRUITS:** Make sure you buy organic fruits when available and keep seasonality in mind. The fruits will be sweeter and your desserts will have a much higher quality.

- **SALT:** Unless otherwise stated in the recipe, I use fine sea salt for baking. It disperses easily into baked goods and also has a clean taste and accentuates the other ingredients without overpowering.

- **SPICES:** Spices tend to go stale if left in the cupboard too long. If you do not know how old a particular spice is, discard it. Whenever possible, use freshly ground or grated whole spices for a deeper and more intense flavor.

- **FLAVORINGS AND EXTRACTS:** These come in many forms such as extracts, liqueurs, and even citrus. You can flavor your baked goods with everything from extracts, like the familiar vanilla and almond, to liqueurs to fresh citrus juices and zest. Make sure you stay away from anything artificial, as it will deeply impact your final product.

- **FATS:** Fats, such as butter and oil, are what give your baked goods tenderness and a moist texture, so always choose high quality products to ensure high quality desserts.

- **DAIRY:** Dairy also provides some fat and moisture. Make sure you use the freshest available and check expiration dates.

- **LEAVENING AGENTS:** Active dry yeast is used to leaven many breads and doughs, and should be proofed in warm water (between 110 and 115°F). It is important to use a thermometer to determine the water temperature, as yeast will not activate in cold water and may die if the water is too hot. Most quick breads do not contain yeast, but utilize other leavening agents such as baking powder and baking soda. Baking soda is used when the recipe calls for acidic ingredients such as buttermilk, sour cream, and citrus. A chemical reaction occurs that helps the dough rise by way of carbon dioxide interacting with the acid in the liquid.

BASIC TIPS AND TECHNIQUES FOR BAKING

Creaming Butter and Sugar

Creaming—or beating together—butter and sugar until light and fluffy ensures the right amount of air is incorporated throughout the mixture and leads to an even distribution of fat and sugar. This means your baked goods will rise properly and have a light texture. Make sure that your butter is at room temperature so that it can blend well with the sugar. Squeeze the side of the butter gently to test for "room temperature" quality. It should be easy to dent, but not melted or runny. If the butter is too cold and you're in a pinch, microwave it in 5 to 8 second increments to achieve a pliable butter.

Place the room temperature butter and the sugar in the bowl of a standing mixer fitted with the paddle attachment and beat them together with the mixer on medium speed until light and fluffy. This should take somewhere between 3 and 5 minutes. (Alternatively, place the ingredients in a bowl and beat them with a hand mixer.) Use a flexible rubber spatula to periodically scrape down the sides of the bowl and then return the mixer to medium speed to make sure the mixture is fully incorporated.

Combining Sugar and Egg Yolks

Combining sugar and egg yolks is best done with a sturdy bowl and a whisk. This is a method of incorporating air into your baked goods. You will know the mixture is ready when the color is pale yellow, which means the sugar has dissolved. When you lift the whisk out of the bowl, the mixture should fall back into the bowl in "ribbons."

Folding Ingredients

Folding ingredients, especially egg whites, can be tricky for even the best of bakers. This will definitely take some practice, but when done correctly, the technique will create light, airy batter that will give your desserts perfect texture. Here are some things to keep in mind: You will want to use a pliable rubber spatula and make light strokes so that you do not deflate the batter. When you start to fold, run the spatula along the side and down to the bottom of the bowl, then gently bring the mixture up and over itself. Continue with the folding process, rotating the bowl a quarter turn each time, until there are almost no streaks in the batter.

Whipping Egg Whites

Whipping egg whites is another one of those tricky techniques in baking, but it's easier once you know some simple tips. First, always use a clean bowl—otherwise, the egg whites will not whip to their fullest potential. Make sure the egg whites are at room temperature. If possible, use a hand mixer or a stand mixer fitted with the whisk attachment. If adding sugar, be sure to add slowly, or else your egg whites could fall and lose volume and lightness. Keep testing to see if the whites have reached your desired peak firmness—soft, medium, or stiff—by stopping the mixer and lifting the whisk out. Finally, be careful not to overwhip the egg whites, as they can become grainy and separate.

Whipping Cream

I recommend using heavy whipping cream because it will have the highest volume and richest taste when whipped. For best results, use a hand mixer or a standing mixer fitted with the whisk attachment, and make sure all the ingredients, bowls, and tools are clean and well chilled. Test for soft, medium, or stiff peaks throughout the whipping process and be careful not to overwhip your cream, as at some point, it will turn into butter.

Melting Chocolate

Fill the bottom of a double boiler with just enough water so it does not touch the double boiler insert when placed on top. (Alternatively, you can use a saucepan and a heatproof bowl that fits snugly over the top, and fill the saucepan with just enough water so it does not touch the bottom of the bowl.) Bring the water to a gentle, low simmer. It is very important that the double boiler insert or bowl does not actually touch the water. It is the heat from the steam that melts the chocolate, not the actual simmering water.

Place the chopped chocolate in the double boiler insert or bowl and place it on top of the water. Stir often until the chocolate is completely melted. Remove the insert or bowl from the heat and allow the melted chocolate to cool slightly before using. Alternatively, place chopped chocolate in a heatproof bowl and microwave it on low in 10 to 15 second intervals, stirring frequently, until the chocolate has melted.

Removing Seeds from a Vanilla Bean

Vanilla bean pods and their seeds give cakes, frostings, pastry creams, ice creams, and cookies the most intense and delicious flavor. To remove the seeds, lay the vanilla bean on a clean work surface and using the sharp tip of a small paring knife, split in half lengthwise, but not cutting all the way through. You will want to expose the center where the seeds are found. With the blade of the knife, carefully scrape out the seeds while holding the bean firmly on the cutting board. Be sure to reserve the pods, which can be used in many ways, such as infusing with sugar, or adding to custards or creams during the cooking process to give more depth and flavor.

Separating Eggs

Have two clean bowls side by side. Gently tap the egg on the side of one of the bowls to crack it. Use your thumbs to open the eggshell. Holding one eggshell half in each hand, keep transferring the yolk back and forth from shell to shell over one bowl, letting the white fall into the bowl until only the yolk is left. Drop the yolk into the second bowl.

Pies and Tarts

Introduction to Pies and Tarts

Whether you are a home cook or professionally trained, there is something so deeply satisfying and pleasurable about baking pies and tarts. From start to finish, I love the process of making, rolling, and crimping the dough, then filling it with decadent and delicious fruits, creams, custards, or chocolate. Comforting, warm, and nostalgic, the recipes that follow conjure up all the best emotions and memories. How can you resist a freshly baked apple pie, with juices bubbling around a golden crust or crumble, beckoning you to dive in? Or a savory Heirloom Tomato Tart (page 26), so colorful with mixed varieties of perfectly ripe and sun-sweetened tomatoes, layered with cheeses and fresh herbs.

The key to making these beautiful creations is to start with the best ingredients, ones that will inevitably give you the best results. Every recipe in this book was developed with seasonality in mind, and I strongly urge you to always use fruits and vegetables that are in season and fully ripened.

Of course, not all recipes on the following pages are sweet—I had to include a few savory favorites such as my Caramelized French Onion Tarte Tatin (page 21). This was the recipe that really made me proud and showed off my skills as a top contender during *The American Baking Competition*. The judges loved the flavor combination of the caramelized onions, thyme, sugar, and sherry vinegar and applauded the triumph of the crust, which was flaky and delicious. It was a tense moment when they were all crowded around my station, forks at the ready and notebooks in hand . . . but their positive reactions—let's call them "raves"— were completely worth the stress.

As one of our esteemed judges made clear week after week, a great pie or tart starts with a great crust. There are a few things to keep in mind when making the crust that will hopefully alleviate some of the worry that comes with the process. First of all, making the dough for the crust should be a very quick process, especially if you have all your ingredients properly measured and well chilled. Use a food processor if you have one, as it will make the process even faster. If the dough seems too dry, add ice water a little at a time until it comes together. You want the dough to hold together but not feel wet or sticky.

Once you have the dough made, wrapped, and properly chilled, roll it out on a lightly floured surface, only using enough flour to keep it from sticking, and brushing off the excess. As you roll out the dough, rotate the round on your work surface a quarter turn at a time. If the dough starts to become sticky and difficult to work with, return it to the refrigerator to chill for 15 to 20 minutes, then try again.

Some recipes will call for you to blind bake a tart or piecrust. The reason you blind bake your bottom crust is that you are going to be filling it with moist ingredients such as fruit, custards, or curds, and you don't want these fillings to make your bottom crust soggy. To blind bake, fit the dough into the tart pan or pie plate, prick it all over with a fork, line it with parchment paper or foil, and then fill it with pie weights (dried beans work, too). Refrigerate the tart shell or piecrust before baking to avoid shrinking. Once the crust has been blind baked (the recipe will specify how long you should keep it in the oven), remove the parchment paper and weights and let it cool before adding the filling and continuing with the recipe.

I encourage you to have fun with these recipes, and feel free to substitute your favorite fruits, custards, curds, and flavorings. Once you nail down the process of making the perfect crust, you will likely find yourself baking pies and tarts for every occasion. They don't call it "easy as pie" for nothin'!

Apple Pie with Walnut-Cinnamon Crumble Topping

Makes one 9-inch pie

This pie has very special meaning for me because my wife's Cuban grandmother, whom I adored, wanted me to make it every time she visited. Mima, as she was affectionately known, held a very special place in the hearts of our entire family, so this recipe is dedicated to her.

Mima had a really spicy personality, kind of like me, so I added a little bit of apple cider vinegar in the crust to give it extra kick! She and I also shared a love for pies with crumble toppings, and this one is so flavorful with cinnamon, walnut, and light brown sugar. Tart apples such as Granny Smith are best for pie recipes because they hold up better during baking and also balance the added sweetness from the sugars.

This pie is super easy and fast to assemble, so it's perfect if you are pressed for time, but still want to make something delicious. I like to serve this with a big scoop of cinnamon or vanilla ice cream, or a big dollop of fresh whipped cream.

FOR THE CRUMBLE TOPPING

· ·

1 cup all-purpose flour

6 ounces walnuts, finely ground

1/3 cup granulated sugar

1/4 cup packed light brown sugar

2 teaspoons ground cinnamon

1/2 teaspoon salt

6 tablespoons (3/4 stick) unsalted butter, cut into pieces and kept cold

FOR THE APPLE FILLING

· ·

8 firm Granny Smith or other tart apples, peeled, cored, and thinly sliced

2/3 cup granulated sugar

2 tablespoons all-purpose flour

2 teaspoons ground cinnamon

2 tablespoons unsalted butter, melted

1 recipe Apple Cider–Spiked Pie Dough (page 191)

Preheat the oven to 375ºF. On a lightly floured surface, roll out the pie dough to a 12-inch circle about 1/4 inch thick. Place the dough in a 9-inch deep-dish pie plate, press in to the bottom and up the sides of the plate, then trim the edges to leave an overhang of about 1½ inches. Tuck the extra dough under around the top of the pie plate and use your fingers to crimp the edges. Chill until ready to use.

Make the crumble topping:

In the bowl of a food processor, combine the flour, ground walnuts, granulated sugar, brown sugar, cinnamon, and salt and pulse. Add the butter and pulse until the mixture forms coarse crumbs. Set the crumble topping aside while you make the filling.

Make the apple filling:

In a large bowl, combine the apples, granulated sugar, flour, cinnamon, and melted butter. Stir until well combined, then mound the filling in the prepared chilled piecrust. Evenly distribute the crumble topping over the filling until completely covered. Cover the pie with aluminum foil and bake for 1 hour, then remove the foil and continue to bake for 20 to 25 minutes more, until the top is crisp and the apples are cooked through.

Apple Strudel

I use store-bought phyllo as the dough for this recipe because these paper-thin sheets are flaky and crisp when cooked and make for a beautiful presentation. Alternatively, you can use store-bought puff pastry or follow my recipe for homemade Puff Pastry on page 185. I started baking apple strudel with my wife's nana, who grew up in Croatia in a large family where cooking was a family affair. I learned the skill of rolling the perfect strudel from her, but have adapted the filling over the years. I like to caramelize the apples first, as it lends them a nice moist texture and enhances the flavor of the fruit. Since winning the competition, I have been appearing across the country on cooking shows; I have made this several times and the hosts have loved it. It is probably one of my most requested recipes.

½ cup (1 stick) unsalted butter

5 Granny Smith apples, peeled, cored, and cut into ½-inch dice

$1/3$ cup plus 2 tablespoons granulated sugar

$1/3$ cup packed light brown sugar

1 tablespoon apple cider vinegar

1 teaspoon ground cinnamon

¼ teaspoon freshly grated nutmeg

1 teaspoon pure vanilla extract

Pinch of salt

10 sheets 9x14 store-bought phyllo dough

Whipped Cream (page 15) or vanilla ice cream, for serving

Preheat the oven to 350°F. Line a baking sheet with parchment paper.

In a large sauté pan, melt 4 tablespoons of the butter over medium heat. Add the apples, ⅓ cup of the granulated sugar, the light brown sugar, vinegar, ½ teaspoon of the cinnamon, the nutmeg, vanilla, and salt and stir to combine. Cook, stirring occasionally, until caramelized, about 20 minutes. Remove from the heat and let cool.

In a small saucepan, melt the remaining 4 tablespoons butter over medium heat. Set aside in a warm place.

Lay 1 sheet of the phyllo vertically on a clean, dry surface, keeping the remaining sheets covered with a towel until ready to use—they will quickly become dry and brittle if left uncovered. Brush the first sheet of phyllo with a thin layer of the warm melted butter, then top with a second sheet of phyllo. Brush it with a thin layer of melted butter and top with a third sheet of phyllo. Repeat until you have stacked and buttered all the phyllo sheets. Place the cooled apples with about ⅓ cup of the juices from the pan across the bottom third of the phyllo stack and start to roll until you form a log. Transfer to the prepared baking sheet, seam-side down, then brush with melted butter and sprinkle with the remaining 2 tablespoons granulated sugar and ½ teaspoon cinnamon. Bake for about 30 minutes or until golden brown. Slice crosswise into rounds and serve with fresh whipped cream or vanilla ice cream.

Apple Tarte Tatin

Serves 6

Baking a tarte tatin can be equally exciting and frightening because you really can't be 100 percent sure how it's going to turn out until you make that final flip. However, when the stars align, the presentation is just as gorgeous as it is dramatic. For this recipe, it's important to cut the apples evenly and in the same way so when the tart is flipped, the top "beauty" side will have a uniform appearance. Try other fruits and even vegetables, such as squash, tomatoes, or caramelized onions (see pages 21 and 93), in place of the apples. The crust is a blank canvas, so let your creative juices flow and be prepared to impress. If you're feeling adventurous, try flipping your tarte tatin in front of your guests at a dinner party—it will add to the excitement!

6 tablespoons (¾ stick) unsalted butter

1 cup plus 1 tablespoon sugar

⅓ cup roughly chopped walnuts

8 large Granny Smith apples, peeled, cored, and quartered

1 teaspoon fresh lemon juice

1 teaspoon ground cinnamon

½ teaspoon freshly grated nutmeg

½ teaspoon pure vanilla extract

1 recipe Classic Pie Dough (page 189)

In a 10-inch heavy-bottomed skillet, melt the butter with 1 cup of the sugar over medium heat. Sprinkle the walnuts over the sugar mixture, then arrange the apples, cut-side up, in the pan over the top. Add the lemon juice and sprinkle with the remaining 1 tablespoon sugar and the cinnamon, nutmeg, and vanilla extract. Simmer the apples until the sugar mixture bubbles and begins to caramelize, about 20 minutes. Remove from the heat and set aside, with the apples still in the pan, to cool.

Preheat the oven to 400°F. On a lightly floured surface, roll out the dough into a ¼-inch-thick round slightly larger than the diameter of your skillet. Cover the cooled apples with the rolled dough, tucking in the edges around the perimeter of the skillet. Bake until the top is golden, 20 to 25 minutes.

Remove from the oven and let cool slightly, then with a small knife, loosen the edges. Place a plate larger than the diameter of the skillet on top of the skillet and, holding the plate and skillet together, carefully invert them so the tarte tatin is unmolded onto the plate.

Banana-Coconut Cream Pie

Banana cream pie has always been my hands-down favorite, but my wife prefers coconut cream pie, so I decided to have a little fun and experiment with the two flavors. The result is this truly magnificent banana-coconut cream pie. The smooth texture and subtle sweetness of the bananas combined with the toasty, crunchy coconut topping is a perfect combination, and is sure to make everyone happy!

1 recipe Classic Pie Dough (page 189)

4 large egg yolks

½ cup sugar

2 tablespoons cornstarch

1½ cups whole milk

1 vanilla bean, split and seeds scraped

2 tablespoons unsalted butter

1½ cups sweetened shredded coconut

½ teaspoon pure vanilla extract

3 ripe bananas, cut into ¼-inch-thick pieces

1 tablespoon fresh lemon juice

Whipped Cream (recipe follows), for serving

Preheat the oven to 375ºF. On a lightly floured surface, roll out the pie dough into a 12-inch round about ⅛ inch thick. Place the dough in a 9-inch pie plate, then trim the edges to overhang by about 1½ inches. Tuck the extra dough under around the top of the pie plate and use your fingers to crimp around the edges. Freeze the dough for about 20 minutes.

Line the dough with parchment paper and fill it with pie weights. Bake for about 20 minutes, then remove the weights and parchment and bake for 7 to 10 minutes more, or until lightly golden. Set aside on a wire rack to cool completely.

In a medium bowl, whisk together the egg yolks, sugar, and cornstarch until smooth; set aside. In a small saucepan, warm the milk and vanilla bean seeds until almost boiling, when small bubbles are starting to form around the edges of the pan. While whisking vigorously, slowly pour the hot milk into the egg yolk mixture and continue whisking until blended, then pour the mixture back into the saucepan. Return the pan to medium heat and cook, whisking continuously, for about 3 minutes, until the mixture begins to boil and thicken. Once it comes to a boil, continue to cook, whisking continuously, for another minute. Remove from the heat and stir in the butter, ¾ cup of the coconut, and the vanilla extract and whisk until the butter has completely melted. Transfer the mixture to a bowl, cover with plastic wrap, pressing the plastic directly against the surface of the mixture to prevent a skin from forming, and set aside to cool to room temperature.

In a medium bowl, toss together the bananas and lemon juice. Arrange the banana slices in the bottom of the piecrust, then pour the cooled pastry cream over the bananas. Cover and chill until set, 4 to 6 hours.

While the pie is chilling, preheat the oven to 350°F. Spread the remaining ¾ cup shredded coconut in an even layer on a rimmed baking sheet and toast in the oven for 8 to 10 minutes or until golden.

Top the pie with whipped cream and sprinkle with the toasted coconut before serving.

WHIPPED CREAM

....

1½ cups heavy cream

⅓ cup confectioners' sugar

1 teaspoon pure vanilla extract

In the bowl of a standing mixer fitted with the whisk attachment, beat together the cream, sugar, and vanilla until it forms stiff peaks. Use immediately or cover and refrigerate for up to 24 hours.

Mini Tartlets with Blueberries and Mascarpone

Makes twelve 3-inch tartlets

I made these beautiful and tasty mini tartlets for the 72 Miniatures Challenge on the finale of The American Baking Competition, *and I was so excited about the results. I love these little pastries; they are incredibly versatile and can be filled with almost any sweet or savory ingredient. A great tip is that you can make the tartlet shells ahead of time and freeze them until you are ready to bake them. Have fun with this recipe and try to come up with unique combinations of flavors—you can even try different fruits. Whatever you decide to fill these with, they are bound to be a hit!*

1 large egg yolk

2 tablespoons ice water

1 teaspoon pure vanilla extract

1¼ cups all-purpose flour

⅓ cup sugar

¼ teaspoon salt

½ cup (1 stick) unsalted butter, cut into pieces and kept cold

1 pint blueberries, plus more for garnish

2 tablespoons light corn syrup

1 cup heavy cream

⅔ cup confectioners' sugar

16 ounces mascarpone cheese

1 pint strawberries, hulled

In a small bowl, stir together the egg yolk, ice water, and vanilla; set aside.

In a food processor, pulse together the flour, sugar, and salt, then add the butter and mix on low speed until the mixture resembles coarse crumbs. Add the egg mixture and mix on low speed until the dough comes together. Turn out the dough onto a lightly floured work surface, shape it into a disc, wrap it in plastic, and refrigerate for at least 30 minutes, or until completely chilled.

Preheat the oven to 350°F.

On a lightly floured surface, roll out the chilled dough to ⅛ inch thick. Cut twelve 4½-inch rounds from the dough and place them in 3- to 3¼-inch tartlet pans. Press the dough so that it is completely fitted into the pans, then trim the edges so that the dough is flush with the top. Use a fork to prick the dough all over and transfer to the refrigerator to chill for 30 minutes. Line each unbaked tartlet shell with parchment paper, fill them with pie weights, and blind bake for about 20 minutes. Remove the parchment and pie weights and bake for 5 to 10 minutes more, or until the crust is lightly golden. Set aside to cool.

Reduce the oven temperature to 300°F. Place the blueberries on a rimmed baking sheet and drizzle them with the corn syrup. Bake for 1 hour. Let cool, then transfer the blueberries to a bowl and mash them and set aside.

In the bowl of a standing mixer fitted with the whisk attachment, beat together the cream and ⅓ cup of the confectioners' sugar until stiff peaks form. Cover and chill until ready to use.

In a separate bowl, beat together the mascarpone and remaining ⅓ cup confectioners' sugar until smooth. Gently fold in the whipped cream. Divide the mixture between two bowls. Fold the mashed blueberries into one of the bowls, then transfer the blueberry whipped cream to a piping bag fitted with a ½-inch star tip.

To assemble, fill each cooled tartlet crust with the plain mascarpone whipped cream mixture. Top each with a hulled strawberry, point-side down (you may need to cut larger strawberries in half horizontally to fit). Fill the hulled center of the strawberry with the blueberry mascarpone mixture and top with fresh blueberries.

White Chocolate and Blueberry Tartlets

Makes twelve 3-inch tartlets

Decadent and delicious, these tartlets are simply irresistible! White chocolate is one of my favorite ingredients because of its rich quality and creamy, smooth consistency. For this recipe, I find that the flavor matches perfectly with the subtle tartness of the blueberries. My daughters are always there to lend a hand, giving the tartlets their finishing touches with ripe, sweet berries and acting as my professional taste-testers to ensure quality! This recipe can be modified to make one 9-inch tart; simply exchange the smaller tartlet pans for one round 9-inch tart pan and proceed with the recipe as follows.

All-purpose flour, for dusting

1 recipe Tart Dough (page 193)

4 large egg yolks

½ cup granulated sugar

3 tablespoons cornstarch

1½ cups whole milk

1 tablespoon heavy cream

½ vanilla bean, split and seeds scraped, pod reserved

Pinch of salt

1 tablespoon unsalted butter

2½ ounces white chocolate, finely chopped

1½ cups fresh blueberries

Confectioners' sugar, for dusting

Preheat the oven to 350ºF.

On a lightly floured surface, roll out the dough to ⅛ inch thick. Cut twelve 4½-inch rounds from the dough, then place them in 3- to 3¼-inch tart pans. Press the dough so that it is completely fitted into the pans, then trim the edges so that the dough is flush with the top. Use a fork to prick the dough all over and transfer to the refrigerator to chill for 30 minutes. Line the unbaked tart shells with parchment paper, fill them with pie weights, and blind bake for about 20 minutes. Remove the parchment and pie weights and bake for 5 to 10 minutes more, or until the crust is lightly golden. Set aside to cool.

In a medium bowl, whisk together the egg yolks, ¼ cup of the granulated sugar, and the cornstarch until smooth; set aside. In a medium saucepan, combine the remaining ¼ cup granulated sugar, the milk, cream, vanilla bean seeds and pod, and salt and bring to a gentle simmer over medium-high heat. While whisking vigorously, slowly pour the hot milk into the egg yolk mixture and continue whisking until blended, then pour the mixture back into the saucepan. Return the pan to medium-high heat and cook, whisking continuously, until the mixture returns to a gentle simmer, 3 to 4 minutes.

Remove the pan from the heat and remove the vanilla pod. Add the butter and white chocolate, stirring until they have completely melted and the mixture is combined. Evenly divide the custard among the prebaked tartlet shells, then cover them with plastic wrap, pressing the plastic directly against the surface of the custard to prevent a skin from forming. Refrigerate until completely chilled and set, about 4 hours.

Top with blueberries and lightly dust with confectioners' sugar before serving.

Caramelized French Onion Tarte Tatin

Makes one 10-inch tarte tatin

I had a lot to prove when I made this recipe on The American Baking Competition—*the stakes were high, and I was ready to establish myself as a top contender. Thankfully, it turned out beautifully, and I was awarded the title of "Star Baker" for the week as well as securing my spot in the finale. Winning this challenge gave me the confidence to successfully finish and ultimately win the competition. This divine tarte tatin tastes like French onion soup, and when flipped, has the elegant appearance of beautifully caramelized onion rosettes. Trust me when I say this recipe is a winner!*

6 tablespoons (¾ stick) unsalted butter

1 tablespoon extra virgin olive oil

1½ teaspoons sugar

2 tablespoons chopped fresh thyme

2 pounds Vidalia onions, peeled and quartered or halved horizontally

2 teaspoons minced garlic

⅓ cup sherry vinegar

1 teaspoon salt

1 teaspoon freshly ground black pepper

½ teaspoon crushed red pepper

All-purpose flour, for dusting

1 recipe Pie Dough with Chives (page 192)

1½ cups grated Gruyère cheese

Crème fraîche, for serving

Preheat the oven to 375°F.

In a 10-inch cast-iron skillet, melt the butter and olive oil together over medium-high heat. Sprinkle the sugar and 1 tablespoon of the thyme over the bottom of the pan, and then add the onions, placing them cut-side down. Cook until the onions are golden brown and caramelized, 10 to 15 minutes. Add the garlic, vinegar, salt, black pepper, crushed red pepper and continue to cook for 10 minutes more, shaking the pan occasionally and reducing heat if necessary to prevent burning. Once the vinegar has almost completely evaporated, remove the pan from the heat and set aside to cool slightly.

On a lightly floured surface, roll out the dough into a ¼-inch-thick round a bit larger than the diameter of the skillet. Cover the onions with 1 cup of the Gruyère and the remaining 1 tablespoon thyme, and then top with the dough round, tucking in the edges around the onions at the perimeter of the skillet. Bake until the top is golden, 25 to 30 minutes.

Remove from the oven and let cool for about 5 minutes. Place a plate larger than the diameter of the skillet on top of the skillet and, holding the pan and plate together, carefully invert them so the tarte tatin is unmolded onto the plate. Sprinkle with the remaining ½ cup Gruyère and serve with a side of crème fraîche.

Chocolate Mousse Tart

I love to make tarts, especially when entertaining, because they are so versatile and simple. In this recipe, the rich, smooth, and chocolaty mousse filling pairs perfectly with the delicate and buttery tart crust. It's not too sweet but has just the right amount of chocolate to balance out the flavors. Once you master the crust, get those creative juices flowing and experiment with flavors and combinations! Make a sweet dessert tart with fillings such as this delicious chocolate mousse, citrus curd, pastry cream, and fruit, or a savory tart for an appetizer, brunch, or side dish with ingredients such as tomatoes, artichokes, roasted vegetables, or cheese. For this recipe, it's best to use a tart pan with a removable bottom. Or, for elegant individual servings, use mini tart pans to make tartlets instead.

2 large egg yolks

1¼ teaspoons pure vanilla extract

¼ teaspoon pure almond extract

¼ cup ice water

1⅓ cups all-purpose flour, plus more for dusting

¼ cup sugar

Pinch of salt

½ cup (1 stick) unsalted butter, cut into pieces and kept cold

8 ounces semisweet chocolate chips

½ cup half-and-half

1 cup heavy cream, cold

Whipped Cream (page 15; optional)

Shaved semisweet chocolate, for decoration (optional)

In a small bowl, whisk together the egg yolks, 1 teaspoon of the vanilla, the al-mond extract, and the ice water; set aside.

In the bowl of a food processor, combine the flour, sugar, and salt and pulse to combine. Add the butter and pulse until coarse crumbs form. Slowly drizzle in the egg yolk mixture until the dough forms a ball. Remove the dough, shape it into a disc, wrap it in plastic, and refrigerate for at least 30 minutes, or until chilled.

Preheat the oven to 375°F.

On a lightly floured work surface, roll out the dough into a circle about 2 inches larger than your tart pan. Flip the dough over onto the rolling pin, then place it over the tart pan. Press the dough to the sides and bottom of the pan, being careful not to stretch it too much or it will shrink when baked. Trim the top edge so that the dough is flush with the top of the pan and refrigerate for about 15 minutes.

Line the dough with parchment paper, fill it with pie weights, and bake for 15 minutes. Remove the weights and parchment and bake until golden, 5 to 8 minutes more. Remove from the oven and let cool completely before filling.

Place the chocolate chips in a small heatproof bowl. In a small saucepan, bring the half-and-half to a boil over medium-high heat and pour it over the chocolate chips, then stir until the chocolate has melted completely and the mix-ture is smooth. Set aside to cool.

In the bowl of a standing mixer fitted with the whisk attachment, or in a bowl using a hand mixer, beat the heavy cream and remaining ¼ teaspoon vanilla until medium peaks form. Immediately fold the chocolate mixture into the whipped cream just until incorporated. Spread the chocolate filling into the cooled tart crust. Refrigerate for 2 hours and up to overnight to set the filling before serving.

To decorate, use a pastry bag fitted with the star tip to pipe whipped cream around the outer edges of the tart. Sprinkle shaved chocolate decoratively in the center of the tart and serve.

Heirloom Tomato Tart

Makes one 9-inch tart

Living in Chicago, we endure extremely cold winters, but all seems right in the world once summer rolls around and the foods of the season become our focus for those few glorious months. Heirloom tomatoes are the culinary highlight of summer for me, and I wait until they are perfectly ripe to make this scrumptious heirloom tomato tart. Red, yellow, green, and purple; I love to combine all the colors and varieties for a beautiful showstopping presentation. With the addition of cheese, herbs, arugula, or even prosciutto or sliced ham, this tart is extremely versatile and can be served as a side dish for an elegant dinner or as a meal on its own. I like to pair this tart with a nice crisp glass of Chardonnay—in fact, I actually submitted this recipe to my favorite vineyard and they featured it on their blog. I was incredibly proud!

¾ cup all-purpose flour

⅓ cup whole wheat flour

Salt and freshly ground black pepper

L cups finely grated Pecorino Romano cheese

½ cup (1 stick) unsalted butter, cut into pieces and kept cold

3 to 4 tablespoons ice water

1 cup shredded provolone cheese

1 cup shredded mozzarella cheese

5 large heirloom tomatoes (use different colors), cut into ¼-inch-thick slices

1 tablespoon chopped fresh thyme

1 tablespoon chopped fresh basil

1 tablespoon chopped fresh oregano

⅓ cup finely grated Parmesan cheese

1 to 2 tablespoons extra-virgin olive oil

¼ cup chopped fresh chives

Preheat the oven to 350°F and place the rack in the center.

In the bowl of a food processor, combine the all-purpose flour, whole wheat flour, a pinch of salt, a pinch of pepper, and the Pecorino and pulse to combine. Add the butter and pulse until the mixture resembles coarse meal, then slowly add 3 tablespoons of the ice water until the dough comes together to form a ball. If the dough is too dry, add more water, 1 teaspoon at a time, until the desired consistency is reached. Press the dough into a 9-inch tart pan and refrigerate for 20 minutes.

Prick holes all over the bottom and up the sides of the chilled crust with a fork, then line it with parchment paper and fill it with pie weights. Blind bake for about 20 minutes, then remove the weights and parchment paper and continue to bake for about 10 minutes more, until golden. Remove from the oven and set on a wire rack to cool completely.

To assemble the tart, arrange the provolone and mozzarella cheeses evenly over the bottom of the cooled tart crust, then layer the tomatoes on top in a circular pattern. Season with the thyme, basil, oregano, and Parmesan and drizzle with olive oil.

Bake until the cheese has melted and the tomatoes are soft, 20 to 25 minutes. Remove from the oven and season with fresh chives and salt and pepper to taste.

Key Lime Pie

Born and raised in Florida, the home of the Key lime pie, my wife is very discerning when it comes to this regionally famous dessert. Thankfully, she was willing to be my professional taste-tester once again as I developed this recipe, and I believe our team-work paid off. It's all about having the perfect balance of tart and sweet without going too far in either direction. In the words of my wife, this Key lime pie is "authentic and absolutely, positively delish!"

7 tablespoons unsalted butter, at room temperature

¼ cup sugar

8 large egg yolks

1¼ cups all-purpose flour

2 tablespoons grated lime zest, plus more for garnish

2 (14-ounce) cans sweetened condensed milk

1 cup Nellie & Joe's lime juice, or substitute fresh lime juice

Whipped Cream (page 15), for serving

Preheat the oven to 400°F.

In a medium bowl, stir together the butter and sugar until well combined, then mix in 1 egg yolk. Add the flour and 1 tablespoon of the lime zest and mix by hand until crumbly. Press the dough into the bottom and up the sides of a 9-inch pie dish. Freeze the dough for about 20 minutes.

Line the dough with parchment paper and fill it with pie weights. Bake for about 20 minutes, then remove the weights and parchment and bake for 7 to 10 minutes more, or until lightly golden. Set aside on a wire rack to cool completely. Leave the oven on.

In a medium bowl, whisk together the remaining 7 egg yolks and remaining 1 tablespoon lime zest until pale yellow. Add the condensed milk and lime juice and continue whisking until combined. Pour into the baked piecrust. Return to the oven and bake until the pie is firm in the center, about 25 minutes. Let the pie cool completely, then refrigerate for at least 1 hour and up to overnight before slicing. Garnish with fresh whipped cream and a sprinkle of lime zest to serve.

Lemon Meringue Pie

Makes one 9-inch pie

For all lemon dessert fans, this one is for you! You'll fall in love with this zesty piecrust filled with rich lemon curd and topped with a gorgeous toasted meringue layer. The lemon curd is thickened with a combination of cornstarch and egg yolks, making it much more stable than other versions. It's important to note that meringue will attract moisture and shrink over time, so this pie is best served the day it's baked.

1 recipe Pie Dough with Lemon Zest (page 190)

4 large egg yolks (reserve whites for meringue)

1 large egg

2 cups sugar

¼ cup cornstarch

1 cup fresh lemon juice

¼ teaspoon salt

4 tablespoons (½ stick) unsalted butter, cut into 1 tablespoon pieces

Finely grated zest of 3 lemons

½ teaspoon cream of tartar

½ teaspoon pure vanilla extract

Preheat the oven to 375°F.

On a lightly floured surface, roll out the dough into a 12-inch circle about ⅛ inch thick. Place the dough round in a 9-inch pie plate, then trim the edges leaving an overhang of about 1½ inches. Tuck the extra dough under around the top and use your fingers to crimp around the edges. Freeze the dough for about 20 minutes. Line the chilled dough with parchment paper and fill it with pie weights. Bake for about 20 minutes, then remove the weights and parchment paper and bake for 7 to 10 minutes more. Set aside to cool.

In a medium bowl, whisk together the egg yolks, whole egg, 1½ cups of the sugar, and the cornstarch until well combined. Whisk in the lemon juice, salt, and ¼ cup water, and transfer the mixture to a heavy saucepan. Bring to a boil over medium-high heat, whisk continuously, then reduce the heat to maintain a simmer and cook until thickened, 2 to 4 minutes more. Remove from the heat and whisk in the butter and lemon zest, then pour the filling into the prebaked crust. Cover with plastic wrap, pressing the plastic gently to touch the surface of the filling, and chill until set, about 2 hours.

Preheat the oven to 375ºF and place the rack in the center.

In the bowl of a standing mixer fitted with the whisk attachment, beat the reserved egg whites and cream of tartar on medium-high speed until soft peaks form and the whisk forms ribbons when lifted out of the bowl. Slowly add the remaining ½ cup sugar and the vanilla, and continue to beat until medium peaks form.

Top the chilled lemon custard with the meringue all the way to the edges to seal the crust; use a rubber spatula to swirl the meringue and create peaks. Bake until the meringue is toasted and lightly browned, 10 to 12 minutes. Remove from the oven and let cool for 25 to 30 minutes before serving.

Raspberry and Dark Chocolate Tartlets

I made these tartlets on The American Baking Competition *during Pies and Tarts Week for the Showstopper Bake, and boy, were they a SHOWSTOPPER! They looked like something straight out of an elegant pastry shop. Since the show, I have been asked to make these over and over again for family and friends. It's always great to have a recipe in your back pocket that you know will not only taste delicious but will also look absolutely beautiful and impressive. This tartlet recipe is the one that does it all! With a flaky crust, layers of sweet raspberry jam and dark chocolate, flavored with Chambord (a black raspberry liqueur), fresh raspberries, toasted almonds, and with a dusting of confectioners' sugar on top, these tartlets will surely become your favorite for parties and entertaining just like they are for me.*

1 recipe Tart Dough (page 193)

8 ounces semisweet (60% cacao) chocolate chips

6 tablespoons (¾ stick) unsalted butter

2 tablespoons light corn syrup

1 teaspoon Chambord

½ cup seedless raspberry jam

8 ounces fresh raspberries

½ cup apricot jam

Slivered almonds, toasted, for garnish

Confectioners' sugar, for dusting

Preheat the oven to 375°F.

On a lightly floured surface, roll out the dough to ⅛ inch thick, then cut out circles 1½ inches greater in diameter than the tartlet pans. Press the dough circles into 12 mini tartlet pans, crimp the top edges, and freeze for about 25 minutes. Line each with a piece of parchment paper or aluminum foil and fill with pie weights, then bake for 15 minutes; remove the parchment paper or foil and weights and bake for about 5 minutes more, or until golden. Set aside to cool.

In a small saucepan, combine the chocolate, butter, corn syrup and Chambord, and stir over medium heat until melted and combined. Set aside.

To assemble, fill each tartlet with 1 tablespoon of the raspberry jam, then top with the chocolate mixture. Let stand at room temperature until set, about 1 hour, then top with fresh raspberries.

In a small saucepan, stir together the apricot jam and 2 tablespoons water. Bring to a boil, then remove from the heat and brush some of the glaze on each tartlet. Top with toasted slivered almonds and dust with confectioners' sugar.

Chicken Potpie

Nourishing, warm, and soul satisfying, almost nothing beats a chicken potpie. As the weather starts to turn cooler in the fall, these pies become a weekly fixture and favorite for family dinners. I love to play with variations by substituting beef short ribs or seafood, or even omitting the proteins and making vegetarian potpies. If you're tight on time, using a store-bought puff pastry or pie dough for the topping instead of making your own is always an option.

When I found out, while competing on The American Baking Competition *in episode one, that making my favorite potpie was the Technical Bake Challenge on the show I was super excited! Once the challenge was revealed I couldn't wait to get started . . . and I actually ended up winning! I topped the pies with a hot-water crust that day, but I'm using puff pastry for this version, which is just as delicious. If you want a faster topping option, you can use a basic pie dough instead.*

4 boneless skinless chicken breasts

⅓ cup olive oil

Salt and freshly ground black pepper

2 russet potatoes, cooked, peeled, and cut into ½-inch dice (about 2 cups)

½ cup (1 stick) unsalted butter

2 Vidalia onions, cut into ½-inch dice

3 carrots, cut into ½-inch dice

¾ cup all-purpose flour

6 cups chicken stock or broth

1 cup half-and-half

10 ounces (1¼ cups) fresh or frozen peas

⅓ cup minced fresh parsley leaves

¼ cup minced fresh tarragon

1 recipe Puff Pastry (page 185) or frozen store-bought puff pastry, such as Dufour

1 large egg, beaten

Preheat the oven to 350°F.

Place the chicken breasts in a glass baking dish or on a baking sheet and coat with the olive oil. Season with salt and pepper to taste. Bake until cooked through, 35 to 45 minutes. Remove from the oven, let cool, and cut or shred into bite-size pieces.

Fill a medium pot with water and bring to a boil over high heat. Add the potatoes and simmer until just cooked through, about 10 minutes. Drain and set aside.

In a large pot, melt the butter over medium heat. Add the onions and carrots and sauté until the onions are translucent and the carrots begin to soften, 8 to 10 minutes. Add the flour and stir for about 1 minute. Stir in the chicken stock, bring to a boil, then reduce the heat to maintain a simmer and cook until thick. Stir in the half-and-half, peas, cooked chicken, potatoes, parsley, and tarragon and season with salt and pepper to taste. Divide the filling among four 6½-inch ovenproof bowls and set aside to cool slightly.

On a lightly floured work surface, roll out the puff pastry to ¼ inch thick. Invert a round bowl slightly larger than your ovenproof bowls onto the dough and, using the bowl as a guide, cut four circles from the dough. Place the pastry rounds over the filled bowls and crimp the edges to seal them, then brush the tops with beaten egg and season with salt and pepper. Using a small sharp knife, make a slit in the top of each potpie to allow steam to escape. Set the ovenproof bowls on a baking sheet and bake until the potpies are bubbly and the pastry is golden brown, about 40 minutes.

Scones, Muffins, and Biscuits

Introduction to Scones, Muffins, and Biscuits

Fresh baked and warm from the oven, homemade quick breads are always the easiest way to make everyone in my family happy. I love making scones, muffins, and biscuits for so many reasons; the process is very straightforward, and having a quick baking project actually helps me relax when I'm feeling a little frazzled. Even if you don't have a ton of time, whipping up a batch of homemade goodies can be as enjoyable as it is cathartic. I think you will be happy to hear that making the recipes in this chapter is likely to be extremely fun and surprisingly simple. Doughs and batters for scones, muffins, and biscuits require very little "fussing" . . . and also very little equipment.

There are a few things to keep in mind when you jump into the recipes on the following pages. For instance, when making Blueberry and Almond Scones (page 41) or Savory Bacon, Cheddar, and Chive Scones (page 44), use a light touch and be careful not to overwork the dough. Remember: Less is more if you want a tender and delicious pastry! Mix the ingredients until they just come together, then lightly pat or roll the dough into shape for cutting. For Southern-Style Biscuits (page 50), make sure your butter is chilled and well distributed in the flour so that you will have flaky, light layers throughout.

Also, don't overmix batter for muffins; instead, mix the ingredients until just combined. If you are adding fruit such as berries, it's best to use a pliable rubber spatula to fold them in at the end. A tip to filling muffin tins is to use an ice cream scoop to portion the batter. Use paper or silicone baking cups to line your muffin tin for easy removal.

Have fun, and don't be afraid to experiment with ingredients for recipes such as Mexican Muffins (page 46) or Savory Bacon, Cheddar, and Chive Scones (page 44). This is your time to relax and bake, so enjoy!

Blueberry and Almond Scones

Makes 6 scones

These blueberry and almond cream scones have a wonderful flaky and cakelike structure. Adding a crunchy, sweet turbinado sugar and almond topping gives the scones such a nice texture and added sweet, nutty flavor. The secret to super-tender scones is to use a light touch with the dough, being careful not to overwork it, which will make them tough. If you choose the food processor method, also be careful not to over-pulse the dough. For an added kick of sweetness, drizzle a bit of lemon glaze on top after baking, and enjoy!

2 cups all-purpose flour, plus more for dusting

1 teaspoon baking powder

½ teaspoon baking soda

$\frac{1}{8}$ teaspoon cream of tartar

¼ teaspoon salt

$\frac{1}{3}$ cup granulated sugar

½ cup (1 stick) unsalted butter, cut into pieces and kept cold

1 cup heavy cream, plus more for brushing

1 large egg

1 pint blueberries

1 cup slivered almonds

3 to 4 tablespoons turbinado sugar

Lemon Glaze (recipe follows)

Preheat the oven to 375°F. Line a baking sheet with parchment paper.

In a large bowl, whisk together 2 cups of the flour, the baking powder, baking soda, cream of tartar, salt, and sugar. Use a pastry cutter or fork to cut in the butter until the mixture looks like coarse crumbs. Add the heavy cream and egg and stir until the dough comes together. Gently fold in the blueberries and ½ cup of the almonds.

Alternatively, in the bowl of a food processor, pulse to combine the flour, baking powder, baking soda, cream of tartar, salt, and granulated sugar. Add the cold butter and pulse until the mixture forms coarse crumbs. Add the heavy cream and egg and pulse just until combined. Transfer the mixture to a large bowl and gently fold in the blueberries and ½ cup of the almonds.

Transfer the dough to a lightly floured surface. Roll or pat the dough into an 8-inch square about ¾ inch thick, then cut it into six 3-inch triangles. Place the scones on the prepared baking sheet. Brush the scones with heavy cream and sprinkle with turbinado sugar and the remaining ½ cup almonds. Bake for about 25 minutes, until golden. Let cool before frosting with the lemon glaze.

LEMON GLAZE

Makes 2 cups

2 cups confectioners' sugar, plus more as needed

3 to 4 tablespoons fresh lemon juice

1 tablespoon half-and-half, plus more as needed

In a large bowl, whisk together all the ingredients until smooth, then drizzle the glaze over baked scones. If the glaze is too thick, adjust the consistency by adding a little more half-and-half. If the glaze is too thin, add more sugar.

Savory Bacon, Cheddar, and Chive Scones

Makes 6 scones

I love to take typically sweet baked goods and turn them into savory treats. In this recipe, crumbled bacon, sharp cheddar cheese, and fresh chives are the stars of these delicious mouthwatering scones. Some mornings I get up extra early to bake these fresh so that my wife, the girls, and I can have them for a weekday breakfast treat. Of course, the aromas of bacon frying and scones baking gets everyone out of bed pretty fast! These are also perfect to serve as a side with soft scrambled eggs, soups, stews, salads, or roasts.

2 large eggs

1 cup buttermilk

3¾ cups all-purpose flour, plus more for dusting

2 tablespoons baking powder

½ teaspoon baking soda

1 teaspoon salt

1 cup (2 sticks) unsalted butter, cut into pieces and kept cold

1½ cups shredded sharp cheddar cheese

½ cup chopped fresh chives

4 slices bacon, cooked and crumbled (reserve 2 tablespoons for topping)

¼ cup whole milk

Preheat the oven to 400 °F. Line a baking sheet with parchment paper.

In a medium bowl, whisk together the eggs and buttermilk, then set aside.

In the bowl of a food processor, combine the flour, baking powder, baking soda, and salt and pulse 2 to 3 times to combine. Add the butter and pulse until it resembles coarse crumbs. Add the eggs and buttermilk mixture and pulse until dough just comes together, then pulse in 1 cup of the shredded cheddar cheese, chopped chives, and all but 2 tablespoons of the bacon (reserve the remainder for topping the scones).

Transfer dough to a lightly floured surface. Roll out or pat the dough into an 8-inch square about ¾ inch thick, then cut into six 3-inch triangles. Place the scones 1 inch apart on the prepared baking sheet.

Brush the tops of the scones with milk, then top with the remaining ½ cup shredded cheddar cheese and reserved bacon. Bake scones until golden brown, 25 to 30 minutes.

Mexican Muffins

Makes 12 muffins

These savory spicy muffins are a stand-alone hit! Chili powder, chiles, and pimentos add kick and a mix of creamed corn, cheese, and bacon gives a boost to the flavor, texture, and taste. Fill a basket with these muffins, place it on the table, and watch them vanish in a flash. They can also be the perfect side to scrambled eggs, salads, or even a nice steak dinner.

Nonstick cooking spray, for the pan (optional)

1¾ cups all-purpose flour

2 teaspoons baking powder

⅛ teaspoon baking soda

¼ teaspoon salt

2 tablespoons sugar

⅛ teaspoon chili powder

1 large egg

½ cup Basic Sourdough Starter (see page 82)

⅓ cup whole milk

1 cup creamed corn

¼ cup canola oil

1 tablespoon canned chopped green chiles

2 tablespoons chopped canned pimentos

½ cup shredded sharp cheddar cheese

2 slices bacon, cooked and crumbled

Preheat the oven to 400ºF. Spray a 12-cup standard muffin pan with nonstick cooking spray or line it with paper liners.

In a medium bowl, whisk together the flour, baking powder, baking soda, salt, sugar, and chili powder. In a separate bowl, whisk together the egg, sourdough starter, milk, creamed corn, oil, chiles, and pimento. Add the wet ingredients to the bowl with the dry ingredients and stir to combine, then fold in the cheese and bacon.

Scoop or spoon the batter into the prepared muffin pan to fill each muffin cup about three-quarters full. Bake until the muffins are golden and a toothpick inserted into the center of a muffin comes out clean, 20 to 25 minutes. Serve warm.

Oatmeal Muffins

Makes 12 muffins

For me, breakfast is the most important meal of the day. I need something that gives me a ton of energy because I am incredibly busy from sunup to sundown. Working, exercising, traveling, cooking, and spending time with my family and friends takes up much of my time, and I need to make sure I feel healthy and energized as much as possible. These oatmeal muffins have become one of my favorite morning snacks; they are simple to make, delicious, and easy to pack when I'm on the move. I usually end up making a double batch so the girls will have enough to take to school during the week as well.

1 cup whole milk

1 cup quick-cooking oats

½ cup raisins

Nonstick cooking spray, for the pan (optional)

1 cup all-purpose flour

1½ teaspoons baking powder

¼ teaspoon baking soda

½ teaspoon salt

½ cup packed brown sugar

$\frac{1}{3}$ cup vegetable oil

½ cup Basic Sourdough Starter (see page 82)

1 large egg, beaten

In a medium bowl, stir together the milk, oats, and raisins and set aside to soak for 1 hour. (Alternatively, if you don't have time to soak the oats and raisins, microwave the mixture for 30 seconds.)

Preheat the oven to 400°F. Spray a 12-cup standard muffin pan with non-stick cooking spray or line it with paper liners.

In a medium bowl, whisk together the flour, baking powder, baking soda, salt, and sugar.

Add the oil, sourdough starter, and egg to the bowl with the soaked oats and raisins and stir well to combine. Stir in the flour mixture and mix until completely blended.

Scoop or spoon the batter into the prepared muffin pan to fill each muffin cup about three-quarters full. Bake the muffins until a toothpick inserted in the middle comes out clean, 20 to 25 minutes. Transfer to a wire rack to cool.

Southern-Style Biscuits

Makes 6 to 8

My wife is from the South, and she loves the foods that remind her of home, so biscuits are a must in my house all year round. The secret to making a great biscuit is to not overwork the dough—just mix until the ingredients come together and the dough is soft, but not wet or sticky. Fluffy, buttery layers on the inside and golden on the outside, these biscuits are great served piled high with sliced ham and grainy mustard, with salty butter and fruit jam for breakfast, or as a side for chili or hearty winter stew.

2 cups all-purpose flour, plus more for dusting

1 tablespoon baking powder

1 teaspoon salt

1/3 cup vegetable shortening, or 6 tablespoons (¾ stick) unsalted butter, cut into pieces and kept cold

1 cup buttermilk

1 to 1 tablespoons heavy cream

Preheat the oven to 450°F. Line a baking sheet with parchment paper.

In a large bowl, sift together the flour, baking powder, and salt three times. Use a pastry blender or fork to cut in the shortening until the mixture resembles coarse meal with pea-size pieces of shortening throughout. Slowly add the milk and mix with a fork or wooden spoon until the dough is combined and holds together.

Turn out the dough onto a lightly floured surface and softly knead it a couple of times to bring it together. Be sure not to overwork the dough, or your biscuits will be tough. Roll the dough into a circle about ¾ inch thick. Using a 3-inch round biscuit cutter, cut out the biscuits and place on the prepared baking sheet. Gather the scraps, reroll them, and continue cutting as many biscuits as possible.

Brush the tops of the biscuits with cream and bake for 12 to 15 minutes, until golden. Serve hot.

Breads and Pizzas

Introduction to Breads and Pizzas

The recipes in this chapter are some of my absolute favorites. I was inspired to start cooking and baking when I was very young, and the first thing I ever learned was how to make bread. My grandmothers were the best mentors—they taught me the importance of "The 3 Ps": precision, patience, and practice. Since those early years as a fledgling baker, I've added many more recipes to my repertoire, and I'm super excited to share them with you.

I love making yeasted doughs and breads, such as Focaccia with Fresh Thyme (page 86), Poppy Seed Sugar Plum Rolls (page 71), or Soft Pretzels (page 77), as they have wonderfully complex textures and flavors and require the most patience and practice. However, it's great to have delicious quick bread recipes on hand—the kind that you can throw together last minute and that require no dough proofing, such as Banana Tea Bread (page 58) or Zucchini and Walnut Quick Bread (page 84).

In recipes that call for kneading the dough, this very important step in the bread-making process helps to build structure and develop texture. By mixing, pushing, and folding, you are releasing the gluten in the flour and also ensuring that the yeast is being evenly distributed throughout the dough. This is what will make your bread rise and bake properly. Here are a few tips and techniques that will help you with the kneading and proofing process.

Using a standing mixer fitted with the dough hook attachment to start the kneading process is very effective and less time-consuming than kneading by hand from start to finish. Once the dough is combined in the mixer, keep the machine running for about 3 to 5 minutes until the dough forms into a ball around the hook. Next, transfer the dough to a lightly floured work surface to finish kneading by hand. Using the heel of your hand, push the dough away from you, then take the far end of the dough and roll it back over the dough closest to you. Rotate the dough a quarter turn clockwise, and repeat, pushing the dough with the heel of your hand and folding it over. Keep repeating until the dough is smooth and elastic, about 8 to 10 minutes.

To prepare for the first proofing, shape the bread dough into a ball and place it in a lightly oiled bowl, then cover the bowl with a clean, slightly damp kitchen towel. Let the dough rise for the amount of time your recipe calls for in a warm (but not hot!), draft-free spot. After the first proofing, the dough should be doubled in size, puffy, and soft when touched.

Some recipes call for you to "punch down the risen dough," which redistributes the yeast and ensures an ample rise during the second proofing. If the dough does not require two proofings, just remove it from the oiled bowl and proceed with the recipe.

If the recipe does require a second rise, punch the dough down first, then shape or place it into an oiled bowl, loaf pan, or baking pan. Cover and let rise again in a warm, draft-free place for the specified length of time.

Keep these simple but important tips in mind as you master the art of making bread, and just remember to be conscious of "The 3 P's": precision, patience, and practice . . . and enjoy the process!

Banana Tea Bread

Makes 1 loaf

Sometimes I get so nostalgic thinking about what a big role my grandmother played in my life. Not only did she teach me how to bake, but she also showed me the value of being a graceful and giving host. From her, I learned that even the smallest gesture could make a person feel welcome in your home. I have such wonderful memories of my grandmother making this super simple but delicious banana tea bread; she was so thoughtful and always had a special little something on hand to offer her family or last-minute guests. She served this bread fresh and warm from the oven, sliced thick with sweet butter melted on top, just as I do to this day!

Nonstick cooking spray or vegetable oil, for the pan

2 large eggs

$2/3$ cup sugar

$1/3$ cup vegetable oil

2 or 3 ripe bananas, mashed

1¾ cups all-purpose flour

2 teaspoons baking powder

¼ teaspoon baking soda

2 teaspoons salt

Preheat the oven to 350°F and place the rack in the center. Lightly coat a 9 x 5 x 3-inch loaf pan with nonstick cooking spray or vegetable oil.

In a medium bowl, whisk together the eggs, sugar, oil, and bananas until combined. In a separate bowl, whisk together the flour, baking powder, baking soda, and salt until combined. Add the flour mixture to the egg and banana mixture and stir until well blended.

Pour the batter into the prepared loaf pan and bake for 55 minutes to 1 hour, until the bread is golden brown and a toothpick inserted into the center comes out clean. Let the bread cool in the pan on a wire rack for about 10 minutes, then invert the pan to remove the bread. Set the bread right side up on the rack and let cool completely.

Sweet Buttermilk Cornbread

Serves 6 to 8

When we first married, my wife, who is from the South, quickly learned what a passionate baker I was. Not missing a beat, she politely requested that homemade cornbread become a staple in our house. Of course I was eager to impress, and after many trials came up with a winner! This version is over the top with flavor and moist texture because of the creamed corn in the batter. To take it to the next level, try adding shredded Jack cheese and roasted green chiles or crisp diced bacon and sliced scallions. The variations are easy and endless!

Nonstick cooking spray or vegetable oil, for the baking dish

1 cup all-purpose flour

1½ cups yellow cornmeal

1 teaspoon salt

2 teaspoons baking soda

¼ cup sugar

1 large egg

1 cup buttermilk or skim milk

¼ cup vegetable oil

1 (10¾-ounce) can creamed corn

1 cup shredded Monterey Jack cheese (optional)

$1/3$ cup canned roasted green chiles, minced (optional)

$1/3$ cup diced cooked bacon (optional)

¼ cup thinly sliced scallions (optional)

Preheat the oven to 400°F. Spray a 9 x 9-inch glass dish or a 9-inch cast-iron skillet with nonstick cooking spray or brush with vegetable oil.

In a large bowl, whisk together the flour, cornmeal, salt, baking soda, and sugar. In a separate bowl, whisk together the egg, buttermilk, oil, and creamed corn. Add the dry ingredients to the wet ingredients and use a wooden spoon or rubber spatula to mix until completely combined; do not overmix. Fold in cheese, chiles, bacon, and scallions, if desired.

Pour the batter into the prepared baking dish and bake until lightly golden and firm to the touch, 25 to 30 minutes, or until a toothpick inserted into the center comes out clean. Let cool slightly in the dish, then serve.

Dinner Rolls

Makes 24 rolls

There's nothing like having fresh, soft, warm dinner rolls as a side with any meal. I mean, seriously, what could be a better sidekick to roast chicken, mashed potatoes, and steamed veggies? Or a big, juicy steak, cauliflower gratin, and creamed spinach? I make heaping baskets of these and serve them with a variety of condiments and fillings such as sweet butter, raspberry jam, sliced ham, and grainy mustard. I also love to make mini burgers, BBQ, or meatball "sliders" with these rolls when I'm hosting casual parties, and believe me, they are always a huge hit!

Butter or nonstick cooking spray, for the baking sheet and bowl

½ cup warm water (110 to 115°F)

1 (¼-ounce) package active dry yeast

2 large eggs

1 cup Basic Sourdough Starter (see page 82)

2 tablespoons sugar

1 teaspoon salt

3 tablespoons unsalted butter, melted

3 to 4 cups all-purpose flour, plus more as needed

Preheat the oven to 400°F. Lightly grease a baking sheet with butter or nonstick cooking spray.

Place the water in a large bowl and sprinkle the yeast evenly over the surface; let sit until foamy, about 5 minutes. Add 1 egg, the sourdough starter, sugar, salt, melted butter, and the yeast mixture and beat to combine. Add 2 cups of the flour and stir until smooth. Add more flour as needed to make soft dough.

Turn the dough out onto a lightly floured work surface and knead it for 5 to 8 minutes. Place in a lightly greased bowl, cover with a clean towel, and set aside to rise in a warm, draft-free place for 2 hours or until doubled in size. Punch down the dough and divide it into 24 pieces. Shape them into balls, place the dough on the prepared baking pan, cover and let rise for 45 to 60 minutes.

In a small bowl, beat the remaining egg and use it to brush the tops of the rolls. Bake 20 minutes, or until golden brown.

English Muffins

Makes 12 to 14 muffins

There is a wonderful little restaurant in my neighborhood that serves the most amazing brunches on the weekends. One of the signature items on their menu is homemade English muffins served as a side with eggs, broiled tomatoes, and house-cured salmon.

They inspired me to create my own recipe, and now these fresh and incredibly tasty English muffins are a mainstay for weekend brunches in my home. I encourage you to also think beyond the traditional Eggs Benedict or morning bread and make individual open-faced tuna melts, croque madames, or our family favorite—English muffin pizzas.

2 tablespoons plus ¼ cup yellow cornmeal

¼ cup warm water (110 to 115°F)

1 (¼-ounce) package active dry yeast

2¾ cups all-purpose flour, plus more for dusting

1 teaspoon baking soda

1 teaspoon salt

1 cup Basic Sourdough Starter (see page 82)

¾ cup buttermilk

2 to 3 tablespoons unsalted butter

Cover a large baking sheet with waxed paper and sprinkle it with 1 tablespoon of the cornmeal. Set aside. In a small bowl, combine the warm water and yeast and set aside until foamy, about 5 minutes.

In a large bowl, combine the flour, ¼ cup of the cornmeal, the baking soda, and the salt. Combine the sourdough starter and buttermilk with the yeast mixture. Using a wooden spoon, stir the wet mixture into the flour mixture until blended.

Turn out the dough onto a lightly floured surface and knead it for 5 to 8 minutes, adding more flour if necessary to keep the dough from sticking. Roll out the dough to ⅜ to ½ inch thick and cut out rounds with a 3-inch round biscuit cutter or a glass. Arrange the rounds on the prepared baking sheet and sprinkle with the remaining 1 tablespoon cornmeal. Cover with a clean towel and set aside in a warm, draft-free place to rise for 45 minutes or until about doubled in size.

Heat a griddle over medium or medium-high heat until a drop of water bounces on the surface. Lightly grease the griddle with the butter and cook the muffins in batches, turning them often, for about 30 minutes. Transfer to a wire rack to cool. Grease the griddle again as needed between batches.

Grandma Griffin's Cinnamon Rolls

Makes 8 rolls

Fresh-baked cinnamon rolls have been a Christmas morning family tradition since I was a little boy. The aromas of butter, cinnamon, and nutmeg fill up every corner of the house and bring back wonderful memories of family and times spent celebrating the holidays together. This recipe makes a soft, rich roll with the perfect balance of spices and sugar.

Tantalizing, sweet, and irresistible, these cinnamon rolls will surely become a favorite in your home. Once when I was little, I woke up early on Christmas Day, and I took the whole batch of cinnamon rolls to my room and hid them! Boy, were my siblings confused and had all sorts of crazy theories about where they had gone. I eventually confessed and brought them out to share with all, but I still kept one hidden for myself . . . how could I resist?

2 cups whole milk

1 (¼-ounce) package active dry yeast

9 tablespoons plus 1 teaspoon granulated sugar

4 to 5 cups all-purpose flour, plus more for dusting

½ cup (1 stick) unsalted butter, melted, plus more for greasing

2 large eggs

1 teaspoon salt

2 teaspoons ground cinnamon

½ teaspoon freshly grated nutmeg

1 cup confectioners' sugar

⅓ cup half-and-half

1 teaspoon pure vanilla extract

In a small saucepan, heat the milk over medium-high heat until it is steaming and small bubbles start to form around the edges. Remove from heat and transfer to a large bowl and let cool to 110–115°F. Add the yeast and 1 teaspoon of the sugar and set aside until foamy, about 5 minutes. Add 2 cups of the flour and stir until smooth and combined. Cover with a clean towel and set aside in a warm, draft-free place to rise for 1 hour.

Punch down the dough, then add 3 tablespoons of the granulated sugar, 2 cups of the flour, ¼ cup of the melted butter, the eggs, and the salt to the risen mixture and mix until a soft smooth dough forms. If the dough seems too loose, add up to 1 cup more flour until the dough is smooth and elastic. Place the dough in a lightly greased bowl, turning it to coat. Cover with a clean towel and let rise 1 hour more.

Grease a 9 x 13-inch baking dish. In a small bowl, combine the cinnamon, nutmeg, and remaining 6 tablespoons granulated sugar; set aside. In a medium bowl, whisk together the confectioners' sugar, half-and-half, and vanilla; set this glaze aside.

On a lightly floured surface, roll out the dough to a 10 x 16-inch rectangle. Brush the dough with the remaining ¼ cup melted butter, then evenly distribute the cinnamon and sugar mixture over the dough. Roll up the dough lengthwise into a log, and then cut it crosswise into eight 2-inch-thick rounds. Place the rounds cut-side up in the prepared baking dish. Cover loosely with a clean towel and let rise for 1½ hours.

Preheat the oven to 350°F. Bake the rolls for 25 to 30 minutes until golden brown. Let cool slightly, then drizzle the warm rolls with the glaze and serve.

Irish Soda Bread

Makes 1 loaf

Irish soda bread is a traditional quick bread that uses the reaction of baking soda and buttermilk as the leavening agent instead of yeast. Although typically associated with St. Patrick's Day, I like to make this simple yet delicious bread year round. In similar fashion to a large scone, the raisins and caraway lend subtle sweetness and a distinctive flavor. For me, this bread is best served fresh baked and warm, with softened salted butter slathered on top. I think you will find a reason to make this bread all year round as well.

Nonstick cooking spray or vegetable oil, for the baking sheet

4 cups all-purpose flour, plus more for dusting

¼ cup sugar

1 teaspoon salt

½ teaspoon baking powder

4 tablespoons (½ stick) unsalted butter, cut into pieces

1½ cups buttermilk

1 large egg

1 teaspoon baking soda

1 cup raisins

2 teaspoons caraway seeds

1 large egg yolk, beaten

4 tablespoons (½ stick) salted butter, softened (for serving)

Preheat the oven to 375°F. Spray a baking sheet with nonstick cooking spray or brush it with vegetable oil.

In a large bowl, whisk together the flour, sugar, salt, and baking powder, then blend in the butter with a pastry cutter or fork until the mixture resembles coarse crumbs.

In a separate bowl, whisk together the buttermilk, whole egg, and baking soda, then add the wet mixture to the dry mixture and stir to combine. Fold in the raisins and caraway seeds.

Turn out the dough onto a lightly floured surface and gently knead for about 5 minutes. Form the dough into a round loaf and place on the prepared baking sheet. Using a sharp knife, score the dough halfway down the loaf and brush the top with the beaten egg yolk. Bake until golden, about 40 minutes.

Poppy Seed Sugar Plum Rolls

Makes 24 rolls

These irresistible rolls, very similar to filled doughnuts, are a tradition in my house every Christmas Eve. The soft dough is stuffed with a sweet poppy seed filling, deep-fried, then coated in sugar—they are over the top in every way! I usually make a big batch so that we have plenty for Christmas morning when the whole extended family starts to arrive for brunch. The same basic recipe can be used with a variety of fillings such as jams, custards, or chocolate. Just fry them and coat with sugar or dust with confectioners' sugar for added sweetness.

2 cups whole milk

1 (¼-ounce) package active dry yeast

2¼ cups plus 1 teaspoon sugar

4 to 5 cups all-purpose flour

4 tablespoons (½ stick) unsalted butter, melted, plus more for greasing

2 large eggs

1 teaspoon salt

1 cup poppy seeds, ground

¼ cup light corn syrup

2 quarts canola oil, for frying

In a small saucepan, heat the milk over medium-high heat until it is steaming and small bubbles start to form around the edges. Remove from heat and transfer to a large bowl and let cool to 110–115°F. Add the yeast and 1 teaspoon of the sugar and set aside until foamy, about 5 minutes. Add 2 cups of the flour and stir until smooth and combined. Cover with a clean towel and set aside in a warm, draft-free place to rise for 1 hour.

Punch down the dough and add 3 tablespoons of the sugar, 2 cups of the flour, the melted butter, the eggs, and the salt to the risen mixture and mix until a soft smooth dough forms. If the dough seems too loose, add up to 1 cup more flour to reach the desired consistency. Place the dough in a lightly greased bowl, turning it to coat. Cover with a clean towel and let rise 1 hour more.

In a small bowl, stir together the ground poppy seeds and 1 tablespoon of the sugar, then add the corn syrup to make a very stiff mixture. If the mixture is too thin, it will leak when the rolls are frying.

Grease a baking sheet and set aside. Pinch off a piece of dough and flatten it into about a 3-inch round. Place about 1 teaspoon of the poppy seed mixture in the middle, bring up the sides of the dough, and pinch them together securely. It should look like a bun. Transfer to the prepared baking sheet and repeat until you have used all of the dough. Cover with a clean towel and let rise for 45 minutes to 1 hour, or until doubled in size.

Place the remaining 2 cups sugar in a brown paper bag; set aside. Heat the canola oil in a large, heavy-bottomed, high-sided pot or deep-fryer until it registers 365°F on a deep-fry or candy thermometer. Working in batches, use a heat-resistant slotted spoon to carefully place the poppy seed rolls in the hot oil. Fry, gently turning with the spoon, until golden brown on all sides. Transfer the rolls to a paper towel–lined plate to drain excess oil. While they are still very hot, transfer the rolls to the bag with the sugar and gently shake to coat. Let cool for 5 minutes, and serve.

Croissants

Makes 16 croissants

With buttery, crisp layers outside and moist tenderness on the inside, freshly made croissants are hard to beat. Mastering the techniques takes some practice and patience, but the results are worth it. It's best to work in stages during the lamination process, which is the technique of layering, folding, and rolling that gives these pastries their distinctive texture and taste. If possible, make and laminate your dough the night before you want to bake the croissants, then all you have left to do is form them into crescent shapes and pop them in the oven when you're ready. It's best to use a butter that is unsalted and has a low moisture content, such as Plugrá, and be sure to keep it cold during the lamination process. These croissants are delicious on their own, but you can take them to another level by filling them with chocolate, fruit, or preserves. You can also make savory croissants with your choice of fillings like ham, cheddar, and chives like I did on The American Baking Competition. *They were devoured immediately after the cameras were off! If adding a filling, increase the baking time by 4 to 8 minutes.*

1¼ cup (2½ sticks) unsalted butter, cold

1¼ teaspoons active dry yeast

3 tablespoons warm water (110 to 115°F)

3 teaspoons sugar, divided

1¼ teaspoons salt

1 cup half-and-half

2½ cups all-purpose flour, plus more for dusting

1 large egg

Place 1 cup (2 sticks) of the butter side by side on a lightly floured work surface and dust the tops with a little flour. Cover with plastic wrap and gently beat down the butter with the side of a rolling pin into a 5 x 7-inch rectangle. Wrap the butter in plastic and refrigerate until ready to use.

In a small saucepan, melt the remaining ¼ cup (½ stick) butter over medium heat; set aside to cool slightly. In a medium bowl, combine the yeast, warm water, and 1 teaspoon sugar. Set aside until foamy, 5 to 8 minutes. Stir in the remaining 2 teaspoons sugar, the salt, half-and-half, and melted butter; set aside.

Place the flour in the bowl of a standing mixer fitted with the paddle attachment. With the mixer running on low speed, add the yeast mixture to the flour until the dough starts to come together. Transfer the dough to a lightly floured surface, knead it gently, and pat it into a rectangle, then roll it into a larger rectangle about ¾ inch thick. Transfer the dough to a baking sheet, cover with plastic wrap, and refrigerate for 45 minutes.

On a lightly floured surface, roll out the chilled dough into a 10 x 12-inch rectangle. Unwrap the chilled butter rectangle and place it in the center of the dough. Fold each corner of the dough to meet in the center to completely cover the butter and seal. Flip the dough package over, sealed-side down, and with the short side facing you, roll it out into a 10 x 24-inch rectangle.

Once rolled, set the dough with one short side facing you. Fold up the bottom third to the center and then take the top third and fold it over that, as if you were folding a letter. Rotate the dough clockwise a quarter turn so the seam side is to your left. Repeat this process of rolling and folding one more time, then cover with plastic wrap and refrigerate for 45 minutes. You will then repeat this process five more times, making sure to refrigerate the dough-and-butter block after each turn (you don't want the butter to soften too much). After the last turn, wrap the dough and refrigerate for at least 4 hours, or up to overnight.

On a lightly floured surface, roll out the chilled block to a 10 x 18-inch rectangle. Cut it in half lengthwise, then cut it crosswise into 4 squares to make 8 squares. Cut each of the squares in half diagonally to make 16 triangles. Roll each triangle lightly from the long end to elongate the point; each should be about 7 inches long. Grab the other two points, and stretch them out slightly as you roll it up. Place the rolled croissants on a baking sheet, tip-side down, curving them slightly. Set aside to rise until puffy and light, 1 to 2 hours.

Preheat the oven to 475°F and place the rack in the top third of the oven.

In a small bowl, beat together the egg and 1 tablespoon water to make an egg wash, then brush it over the tops of the croissants. Bake until golden brown and flaky, 12 to 15 minutes.

FRANGIPANE CROISSANT FILLING

1 cup whole almonds, toasted

¼ cup packed light brown sugar

½ teaspoon ground cinnamon

2 tablespoons all-purpose flour

2 tablespoons unsalted butter

1 large egg

In the bowl of a food processor, combine the toasted almonds and the sugar and pulse until coarse. Add the remaining ingredients and process to make a paste. Follow the directions for plain croissants on page 73, adding 1 tablespoon of the filling to the center of the dough triangles before rolling them into croissants. Bake, adding 4 to 8 minutes to the baking time indicated above.

HAM, CHEDDAR, AND CHIVE CROISSANT FILLING

1 cup grated sharp cheddar cheese

$1/3$ cup sliced fresh chives

1 cup diced ham

Follow the directions for plain croissants on page 73, dividing the cheese, chives and ham evenly among the dough triangles before rolling them. Bake, adding 4 to 8 minutes to the baking time indicated above.

Soft Pretzels

I was pretty excited when they announced in week 4 of The American Baking Competition *that we would be making pretzels for the Technical Bake Challenge. I had a technique combining proofing, boiling, and then baking the dough that is tried and true, and I was ready to show the judges I was in the competition to win. Soft on the inside, golden, slightly crisp, and salty on the outside, these pretzels are absolutely amazing right out of the oven. I have an Oktoberfest party every year and serve these fresh baked with lots of mustards and warm cheese sauce. I also love to make my now famous "pretzel dogs" by forming the pretzel dough around German sausages or franks, then brushing them with egg wash, salting, and baking. They are always a huge hit!*

1½ cups warm water (110 to 115°F)

1 tablespoon sugar

2 teaspoons kosher salt

4 tablespoons (½ stick) unsalted butter, melted

1 (¼-ounce) package instant dry yeast

4½ cups bread flour

Olive oil, for greasing

⅔ cup baking soda

2 large egg yolks

½ cup pretzel salt or coarse salt

In the bowl of a standing mixer fitted with the dough hook, combine the warm water, sugar, kosher salt, butter, yeast, and flour and mix on medium-low speed until a dough forms, 3 to 5 minutes. Remove the dough from the bowl and knead it on a lightly floured surface for another minute, then place it in a large, lightly greased bowl, turning it to coat. Cover with a towel and set aside in a warm, draft-free place to rise until doubled in size, about 45 minutes.

Preheat the oven to 450°F and place the rack in the center.

In an 8-quart pot, bring 10 cups water and the baking soda to a rolling boil. In a small bowl, beat the egg yolks with 2 teaspoons water to make an egg wash; set aside.

Turn out the dough onto a lightly oiled work surface and divide it into eight equal pieces. Roll each piece into a 24-inch rope. Make a U shape with the rope. Holding the ends of the rope, cross them over each other and press them to the bottom of the U to form a pretzel shape.

Working in batches, carefully place the pretzels into the boiling water and boil for 30 to 35 seconds each. Remove them from the water, drain briefly on a towel, then transfer to a baking sheet (you may need to use more than one). Brush the tops with the egg wash and sprinkle each with 1 tablespoon of the pretzel salt. Bake until deep golden brown in color, 12 to 14 minutes. Serve immediately.

Sourdough Bread

Makes 2 loaves

The perfect sourdough bread is not difficult to make; it just takes a little bit of time, practice, and patience. The best way to really learn the process is to make it on a regular basis and understand that the yeast in sourdough can be affected from house to house based on environment and climate conditions. The starter and sponge mixture give the bread its distinctive flavor, texture, and complexity. Once you have mastered the art of making the starter, I'm confident that you will master the art of making fantastic sourdough bread time and time again. Fresh sourdough bread was one of the most requested items from my great-grandma Mae's bakery, and apparently the neighbors would see my grandpa in the morning riding his bike all over the city with bread stacked so high he could barely see over his basket. I just know he snuck an extra loaf out of the bakery with him to snack on for those long bike rides and deliveries, and who could blame him!

FOR THE SPONGE

1 cup Basic Sourdough Starter (see page 82)

2 cups warm water (110 to 115°F)

2½ cups all-purpose flour

FOR THE BREAD

· ·

1 cup whole milk

3 tablespoons unsalted butter

2 tablespoons sugar

2 teaspoons salt

1 (¼-ounce) package active dry yeast

¼ cup warm water (110 to 115°F)

6 to 7 cups all-purpose flour

Make the sponge:

In a large bowl, combine the sourdough starter, warm water, and flour. Mix thoroughly to form a dough, cover with plastic wrap or towel, and let stand in a warm place for about 8 hours or overnight.

Make the bread:

In a medium saucepan, heat the milk over medium-high heat until just beginning to boil, then remove from the heat and stir in the butter, sugar, and salt. Set aside to cool for about 10 minutes.

In a small bowl, combine the yeast with the warm water. Let stand until frothy, about 5 minutes. Stir milk mixture and the yeast into the prepared sponge, then add 3 cups of the flour. Stir with a wooden spoon to make a soft dough. Transfer the dough to a lightly greased bowl, cover with a clean towel, and set aside in a warm, draft-free place to rise for 40 to 45 minutes, until doubled in size.

Add enough of the remaining flour to make a medium to stiff dough. Turn out the dough onto a lightly floured surface and knead it for 5 to 7 minutes, until it is smooth and elastic. Transfer the dough to a bowl, cover with a clean towel, and let rest for about 10 minutes.

Grease two 9 x 5-inch loaf pans. Divide the dough equally, gently shape each piece into a loaf shape, and set the loaves into the prepared pans. Cover and let rise until doubled in size and reaching the tops of the pans, about 1 hour. Do not let the dough rise above the tops of the pans, or it will be overproofed.

Preheat the oven to 375ºF and place the rack in the center of the oven. Bake until golden and cooked through, 45 to 50 minutes. Cover with aluminum foil if the tops of the loaves start getting too dark. Remove the loaves from the pans and let cool on a wire rack.

Basic Sourdough Starter

My grandmothers were very passionate about bread making, and as a child I used to watch them intently, anxious to absorb their techniques and imitate their skills. I learned that they often used a sourdough "starter," which helps leaven the bread and imparts a unique flavor and structure. My recipe for a basic starter is one that you can make ahead and use when needed. I know it may seem time-consuming, but the recipe is simple, and if you want really delicious bread, I think you will find it's worth the effort.

2 cups all-purpose flour, plus more flour as needed to feed the prepared starter

3 tablespoons sugar

1 (¼-ounce) package active dry yeast

2 cups warm water (110 to 115°F)

½ teaspoon salt

In a large bowl, combine all the ingredients and beat with a wooden spoon. Cover the bowl with a clean towel or plastic wrap and set aside in a warm, draft-free place. Let the starter ferment for 2 to 3 days, stirring it several times each day. If the dough bubbles and has a nice sour smell, then you have attracted the good bacteria and airborne yeast that will give your sourdough bread its flavor. If the color is slightly pink and the starter smells moldy, discard it and start over. After it has fermented, transfer the starter to a plastic container with a lid that has an air vent and refrigerate it until ready to use.

You will need to feed and replenish your starter depending on how often you use it. If you do not use your starter often, you will need to repeat the feeding process every day for 3 days before using the starter.

When you remove the starter from the refrigerator, pour off any liquid that has collected. Check your starter again for color and smell: If it smells moldy and the color is off (slightly pink), discard it and start over. If everything looks and smells okay, stir in ½ cup all-purpose flour and ⅓ cup cool water to make a dough that has the consistency of a thin batter. Cover and let the batter stand at room temperature overnight before placing it back into the refrigerator until ready to use.

Tip: If your starter is very tangy and you only want a mild sourdough flavor, add ½ teaspoon baking soda with the flour when you make yeast breads.

Zucchini and Walnut Quick Bread

Makes 2 loaves

Baking bread is a huge passion of mine, something I take great pride in. I enjoy the process of making the dough, waiting for it to rise, shaping it, and baking it almost as much as I enjoy eating it. However, as much as I love it, there are occasions when I just don't have the time. Quick breads are perfect for those moments, as they do not use yeast and therefore do not require a rising time. Instead, they rise while baking because of leavening agents such as baking powder and baking soda. This quick bread with grated zucchini and walnuts is so flavorful and moist, it will be a recipe you will want to use time and time again.

Nonstick cooking spray or vegetable oil, for the pan

2 medium zucchini, unpeeled, halved and seeded

3 large eggs

2 cups sugar

1 cup vegetable oil

2 teaspoons pure vanilla extract

3 cups all-purpose flour

¼ teaspoon baking powder

1 teaspoon baking soda

1 teaspoon salt

2 teaspoons ground cinnamon

1 cup chopped walnuts

Preheat the oven to 325°F and place the rack in the center of the oven. Lightly coat two 9 x 5 x 3-inch loaf pans with nonstick cooking spray or vegetable oil.

On the large holes of a box grater, grate the zucchini until you have 2 cups; set aside.

In a large bowl, whisk together the eggs, sugar, oil, and vanilla. In a separate medium bowl, whisk together the flour, baking powder, baking soda, salt, and cinnamon. Add the flour mixture to the egg mixture and stir until well combined, then stir in the grated zucchini and chopped nuts.

Evenly divide batter between the prepared pans. Bake until a toothpick inserted into the center of each loaf comes out clean, 50 to 60 minutes. Let cool in pans for about 10 minutes, then invert to remove the loaves from the pans. Set the loaves right-side up on a wire rack and let cool completely.

Focaccia with Fresh Thyme

Serves 6 to 8

I remember the first time I tasted truly delicious focaccia bread on a trip to New York's Little Italy with my wife. It was so simple, seasoned with extra-virgin olive oil, sea salt, and fresh thyme, and we couldn't get enough. We even returned to the same restaurant the next night just to have more of that delicious bread. Similar to a pizza dough but made with more leavening, focaccia should be a bit thicker and have indentations on the top which allow the olive oil to soak into the bread and also help with the bubbling of the dough during the baking process.

Olive oil is brushed on top before the dough rises in order to preserve moisture and give the bread a soft texture with slightly crisp top. When I want to make variations to the original recipe, I like to add thinly sliced tomatoes, Italian olives, sliced pepperoni, or caramelized onions with garlic and fennel seed (see recipe opposite) on top before baking.

Cut the focaccia into big squares for your dinner bread basket, split it lengthwise and use it for sandwiches, or cut it into cubes, toast, and use as croutons in salads. Any way you like . . . Tutti mangia!

1 cup warm water (110 to 115°F)

1 teaspoon sugar

1 (¼-ounce) package active dry yeast

3 cups all-purpose flour

½ teaspoon fine sea salt

¼ cup extra-virgin olive oil, plus more for greasing

¼ cup chopped fresh thyme

Coarse sea salt, for sprinkling

In a small bowl, combine the sugar with the warm water and stir to dissolve. Sprinkle with the yeast and stir, and set aside until foamy, 8 to 10 minutes.

In the bowl of a standing mixer fitted with the dough hook, combine the flour and fine sea salt. Add the olive oil, thyme, and yeast mixture. With the mixer on medium speed, knead until the dough comes together and is smooth, about 5 minutes. Turn out the dough into a lightly oiled bowl and brush the top with oil. Cover the bowl completely with a clean towel and set aside in a warm, draft-free place to rise for 50 minutes to 1 hour.

Grease a baking sheet. Punch down the dough, turn it out onto the prepared baking sheet, and spread it into a rectangle. Brush the top with olive oil, cover with a clean towel, and let rise for another hour.

Preheat the oven to 450ºF. Dimple the dough evenly all over the top with your fingertips. Brush with olive oil and sprinkle with coarse sea salt. Bake for 20 to 30 minutes until golden.

CARAMELIZED ONION, GARLIC, AND FENNEL SEED FOCACCIA TOPPING

¼ cup olive oil

1 medium yellow onion, thinly sliced

1 tablespoon sugar

2 cloves garlic, minced

2 teaspoons fennel seeds

Sea salt and freshly ground black pepper

In a medium sauté pan, heat the olive oil over medium heat. Add the onion and sugar and cook until the onion is lightly browned and caramelized, about

15 minutes. Add ⅓ cup water to deglaze the pan and cook until the water has evaporated completely, 1 to 2 minutes. Add the garlic, fennel seeds, and salt and pepper to taste and cook for about 2 minutes more. Prepare the focaccia as directed on page 87, evenly distributing the onions over the dough just before baking.

Chicago-Style Deep-Dish vs. New York–Style: Brian's Pizza Two Ways

Serves 4

So there is always a big debate in this country: What's better, Chicago-style pizza or New York–style pizza? Chicago Deep-Dish has a thicker crust and loads of gooey cheese on the bottom and sauce on top, while New York–Style has a thin and crispy crust with the cheese on the top and sauce on the bottom. Of course I have a bias for Chicago because I have to give props to my hometown. But I will say, I have had—and I make—an equally good New York–style pizza! Both recipes are absolutely perfect for pizza-night parties with family and friends. I always have a variety of meats and veggies, such as pepperoni, onions, peppers, mushrooms, and olives on hand so each person can choose what they want. Everyone is happy to help load on toppings and then dive in once the pizzas have the perfect crisp, golden crust and bubbling cheeses and toppings. Delicious!

CHICAGO-STYLE DEEP-DISH PIZZA

Makes one 16-inch deep-dish pizza

For best results, I like to use a deep-dish pizza pan, but you can also use a 9 x 13-inch baking dish. The trick to getting that thick, crispy crust is double proofing the dough before baking.

1 teaspoon sugar

1 cup warm water (110 to 115°F)

1 (¼-ounce) package rapid rise yeast

2 cups all-purpose flour

1 cup fine cornmeal (all-purpose flour can be substituted)

¼ cup olive oil, plus more as needed

Pinch of salt

4 cups grated mozzarella cheese

Toppings of your choice

½ cup finely grated Parmesan cheese

1 (28-ounce) can crushed tomatoes with basil

In a small bowl, combine the sugar with the warm water and stir to dissolve. Sprinkle with the yeast, stir, and set aside until foamy, 5 to 8 minutes.

In the bowl of a standing mixer fitted with the dough hook, combine the flour and cornmeal. Add the olive oil, salt, and yeast mixture. With the mixer on medium speed, knead until the dough comes together and is smooth, about 5 minutes. Turn out the dough into a lightly oiled bowl and brush the top with oil. Cover the bowl completely with a clean towel and set aside in a warm, draft-free place to rise for about 45 minutes.

Punch down the dough and transfer it to a 14-inch deep-dish pizza pan, spreading it halfway up the sides of the pan. Cover with a clean towel and let rise for about 40 minutes, until puffed.

Preheat the oven to 450°F. Press the dough completely up the sides of the pan, then spread the mozzarella evenly over the bottom. Now is the time to add your favorite toppings! Spread them evenly over the dough, then drizzle olive oil around the edges and over the top and sprinkle evenly with the Parmesan. Spread the crushed tomatoes evenly over the top.

Bake for 20 to 25 minutes, until the cheese is bubbling and the crust is golden.

New York–Style Pizza

Makes two 16-inch pizzas

1 teaspoon sugar

1 cup warm water (110 to 115°F)

1 (¼-ounce) package rapid rise yeast

3 cups all-purpose flour, plus more for dusting

¼ cup olive oil, plus more for greasing

Pinch of salt

Cornmeal, for dusting

1 (28-ounce) can crushed tomatoes with basil

Caramelized Onions with Mushrooms (recipe follows)

¼ cup grated Parmesan cheese

1 to 2 tablespoons Italian herb blend

1 cup grated fontina cheese

1 cup grated mozzarella cheese

12 to 16 slices pepperoni

In a small bowl, combine the sugar with the warm water and stir to dissolve. Sprinkle with the yeast, stir, and set aside until foamy, about 5 minutes.

In the bowl of a standing mixer fitted with the dough hook, combine the flour, olive oil, salt, and yeast mixture. With the mixer on medium speed, knead until combined and smooth, about 5 minutes. Turn out the dough into a lightly oiled bowl and brush the top with oil. Cover the bowl completely with a towel and let rise for about 45 minutes.

Preheat the oven to 475°F. Brush two rimless 16-inch pizza pans with olive oil and sprinkle with cornmeal.

Punch down the dough and divide it into two equal pieces. On a lightly floured surface, use your palm to roll each piece into a ball, then use a rolling pin to roll out the balls until the dough is ultra-thin, about ¼ inch thick. Place the rolled dough on the pans and brush with olive oil. Divide the crushed tomatoes, caramelized onions with mushrooms, and Parmesan evenly between the pizzas. Season with the herb blend and then top evenly with the fontina, mozzarella, and pepperoni.

Bake for about 20 minutes, or until the cheese is bubbling and the crusts are lightly browned, turning the pans halfway through so they cook evenly.

CARAMELIZED ONIONS WITH MUSHROOMS

2 tablespoons olive oil

1 large onion, thinly sliced

1 teaspoon sugar

Salt

8 ounces button mushrooms, thinly sliced

Freshly ground black pepper

In a medium skillet, heat the olive oil over medium heat. Add the onion, sugar, and a pinch of salt. Cook, stirring occasionally, until the onions start to turn golden brown, about 15 minutes. Add ¼ cup water, stir to loosen any browned bits from the bottom of the pan, and simmer for about 5 minutes, or until the onions are soft and caramelized. Stir in the mushrooms and continue to cook until just soft, 2 to 3 minutes. Season with salt and pepper to taste.

Stromboli

Serves 4 to 6

Have you ever walked by a pizza joint that displays their menu items in the window? If you are anything like me, the stromboli is generally the one that catches your eye. Big pizza turnovers stuffed with hot melted cheese, sausage, salami, or pepperoni . . . my mouth is watering just writing about it. I love to serve these with fresh homemade marinara sauce for dipping, extra crushed red pepper, and freshly grated Parmesan cheese to make it an even more authentic experience. The tomato, rosemary, and fennel topping bakes into the dough and gives it a fresh and herbaceous kick. You can make it your own by mixing up the meats and cheeses, as well as the toppings. My best friend, Mike, is addicted to these. If I tell him I'm making stromboli, he inevitably shows up at my house with a bottle of wine, ready to eat. Who can blame him?

1 teaspoon sugar

1 cup warm water (110 to 115°F)

1 (¼-ounce) package instant yeast

3 cups bread flour, plus more for dusting

¼ cup plus ⅓ cup extra-virgin olive oil

Pinch of salt

8 ounces Genoa salami, thinly sliced

8 ounces smoked mozzarella cheese, thinly sliced

8 ounces provolone cheese, thinly sliced

⅓ cup torn fresh basil leaves

1 tablespoon minced garlic

1 pint cherry tomatoes, halved

1 teaspoon fennel seeds

1 tablespoon chopped fresh rosemary

½ teaspoon crushed red pepper (optional)

Sea salt and freshly ground black pepper

In a small bowl, combine the sugar with the warm water and stir to dissolve. Sprinkle with the yeast, stir, and set aside until foamy, about 5 minutes.

In the bowl of a standing mixer fitted with the dough hook, combine the flour, ¼ cup of the olive oil, the salt, and the yeast mixture. With the mixer on medium speed, knead until the dough is combined and smooth, about 5 minutes. Turn out the dough into a lightly oiled bowl and brush the top with oil. Cover the bowl completely with a clean towel and set aside in a warm, draft-free place to rise until doubled in size, about 1½ hours.

Preheat the oven to 375ºF. Brush a baking sheet with olive oil.

Punch down the dough and let sit for about 15 minutes to relax.

Turn out the dough onto a lightly floured surface and roll it into an oval about 22 inches long and 12 inches wide. Position the dough with one short end of the oval facing you. Layer the salami, mozzarella, provolone, and basil in the center of the dough up to 6 inches wide, leaving 3 inches on either long side. Fold down about 1 inch of the dough at the top end. Then, using a sharp knife, cut 1¼-inch slashes on an angle along each long side of the dough. Alternating sides and starting at the top, fold these flaps over the filling to form a crisscrossing "braid" of dough. Fold the bottom end of the oval over the last few strips to seal. Use a wide metal spatula to transfer the stromboli to the prepared baking sheet.

In a medium bowl, toss together the garlic, tomatoes, fennel seeds, rosemary, crushed red pepper, remaining ⅓ cup olive oil, and salt and black pepper to taste. Spoon the mixture over the stromboli, cover with plastic wrap, and let sit for 20 minutes. Remove the plastic wrap, then bake for 45 minutes until golden brown.

Cookies, Bars, Biscotti, and Brownies

Introduction to Cookies, Bars, Biscotti, and Brownies

Okay, I admit it—I'm obsessed with cookies, which is exactly how I got the nickname Cookie Monster. My over-the-top passion for cookies inspires me to fill our big cookie jar to the brim with delicious treats on a daily basis. I find it so calming and delightfully easy to pull together the ingredients to whip up a quick batch of Orange Oatmeal Chews (page 121), Gingersnaps (page 117), or Salted Peanut Cookies (page 127). The best part is, I rarely need to make a store run as most of the ingredients I need are already in my pantry.

Nothing makes my kids happier than coming home from school and smelling fresh-baked cookies or finding Double Chocolate Brownies (page 115) in the oven. I think we all can appreciate the absolute joy that comes from that experience; it takes us back to a place and time that is wonderfully simple and comforting. I grew up in a house with four brothers and sisters, and my mom was diligent about baking us amazing treats every day. It's a tradition that I'm incredibly happy and excited to pass along to my own kids. When I have a little extra time, I'll make a few varieties of cookie dough, wrap them, and store them in the fridge so that I can bake them off throughout the week.

Some of the recipes in this chapter require a bit more time and precision, such as the macarons (pages 108, 111, and 113) and the Chocolate-Cherry Biscotti (page 105), but the beauty, texture, and taste of these cookies make them worth the extra effort. I love to find festive and decorative tins or packaging to wrap these as gifts for birthdays, party favors, or special occasions.

LEFT: Banana-Coconut Cream Pie (page 13)
PHOTOGRAPHY BY MARK FERRI PHOTOGRAPHY

RIGHT: Heirloom Tomato Tart (page 26)
PHOTOGRAPHY BY MARK FERRI PHOTOGRAPHY

LEFT: Lemon Meringue Pie (page 30)
PHOTOGRAPHY BY MARK FERRI PHOTOGRAPHY

ABOVE: Raspberry and Dark Chocolate Tartlets (page 32)
PHOTOGRAPHY BY MARK FERRI PHOTOGRAPHY

LEFT: Grandma Griffin's Cinnamon Rolls (page 66)
PHOTOGRAPHY BY MARK FERRI PHOTOGRAPHY

LEFT: Croissants with Ham, Cheddar, and Chive filling (pages 73, 76)
PHOTOGRAPHY BY MARK FERRI PHOTOGRAPHY

ABOVE: Soft Pretzels (page 77)
PHOTOGRAPHY BY MARK FERRI PHOTOGRAPHY

LEFT: Chicago-Style Deep-Dish Pizza (page 90)
PHOTOGRAPHY BY MARK FERRI PHOTOGRAPHY

LEFT: Brian's Famous Cakey
Chocolate Chip Cookies (page 101)

RIGHT: Chocolate-Cherry Biscotti (page 105)

LEFT: Chocolate-Espresso Macarons (page 108)
PHOTOGRAPHY BY MARK FERRI PHOTOGRAPHY

ABOVE: Pumpkin Bars (page 125)
PHOTOGRAPHY BY MARK FERRI PHOTOGRAPHY

LEFT: Berry Trifle Cake (page 134)
PHOTOGRAPHY BY MARK FERRI PHOTOGRAPHY

RIGHT: Carrot Cake with Maple-Mascarpone Frosting (page 141)

LEFT: Cheesecake with Caramel-Apple Topping (page 144)

LEFT: Chocolate Layer Cake with Chocolate Buttercream Frosting (page 152)
PHOTOGRAPHY BY MARK FERRI PHOTOGRAPHY

RIGHT: Orange-Almond Dacquoise (page 164)
PHOTOGRAPHY BY MARK FERRI PHOTOGRAPHY

Brian's Famous Cakey Chocolate Chip Cookies

These cookies are my trademark, which is why, with all modesty, I've aptly named them Brian's Famous Cakey Chocolate Chip Cookies! Okay . . . so I actually have my dear, amazing mom to thank for this "famous" recipe of mine—she used to make the same dough into bar cookies, and called them Chocolate Cheevies. Whatever the name, I know I cannot even think about having a party or gathering without serving these.

2¼ cups all-purpose flour

½ teaspoon baking soda

¼ teaspoon baking powder

½ teaspoon salt

14 tablespoons (1¾ sticks) unsalted butter, at room temperature

¾ cup granulated sugar

¼ cup packed light brown sugar

2 large eggs

1 teaspoon pure vanilla extract

½ teaspoon pure almond extract

1 cup semisweet chocolate chips

1 cup 60% cacao chocolate chips

Preheat the oven to 350°F. Line two baking sheets with parchment paper.

In a small bowl, whisk together the flour, baking soda, baking powder, and salt and set aside.

In the bowl of a standing mixer fitted with the paddle attachment, cream together the butter and both sugars on medium speed until light and fluffy, 2 to 3 minutes. Add the eggs, vanilla, and almond extract, and beat until well combined, about 1 minute. Reduce the speed to low and add the flour mixture, mixing until just combined. Stir in the chocolate chips.

Use a 2-inch ice cream scoop or heaping tablespoon and drop the dough about 2 inches apart on the prepared baking sheets. Bake until the cookies are golden around the edges and set in the center, 10 to 12 minutes. Remove from the oven and let cool on the baking sheets for 1 to 2 minutes. Transfer to a wire rack and let cool completely.

Mini Pavlovas with White Chocolate–Coated Popcorn

These decadent mini pavlovas were one of the three 72 Miniatures that I made for the finale of The American Baking Competition. *We each had to pick a food that represents our home state and somehow incorporate that food into one of the three desserts. After much research, I found out that in 2004, the state snack food for Illinois was popcorn. When I was developing this recipe, I thought, "How cool would it be to make little bags of popcorn?" So I made mini pavlovas and filled them with sweetened whipped cream. Then I coated popcorn with red, white, and blue chocolate. The judges absolutely loved these, and they definitely helped ensure my win!*

6 large egg whites

½ teaspoon cream of tartar

2 cups sugar

12 ounces white chocolate, chopped

1²/₃ cups heavy cream

Red and blue food coloring

1 to 2 cups freshly popped popcorn

Preheat the oven to 300°F. Line a baking sheet with parchment paper.

In the bowl of a standing mixer fitted with the whisk attachment, whisk the egg whites on medium speed until foamy. Add the cream of tartar, then with the mixer running, slowly add the sugar and continue to whisk until glossy, stiff peaks form. Transfer the mixture to a piping bag fitted with a medium, ½-inch round tip. Pipe dollops of the meringue approximately 1½ inches wide on the prepared baking sheet, leaving about 2 inches between each. Next, pipe meringue around each dollop twice, creating a well to hold the filling. Place in the oven and turn off the heat. Leave to dry for 2 to 3 hours. Remove from the oven and let cool completely on the baking sheet.

Place the white chocolate in a medium heatproof bowl and set aside. In a small saucepan, heat ⅓ cup of the heavy cream until small bubbles start to form around the edges, then pour the hot cream over the chocolate and mix until completely smooth and combined. Divide the chocolate mixture between three small bowls. Add a few drops of red food coloring to one bowl, a few drops of blue to another, and leave third bowl white. Coat 3 pieces of popcorn for each pavlova, dipping 1 in the white chocolate, 1 in the blue, and 1 in the red. Set aside to harden on a parchment-lined baking sheet or plate.

In a large bowl, whisk the remaining 1⅓ cups cream until stiff, then fill each pavlova with the whipped cream. Stack the coated popcorn (one each of red, white, and blue) on top of each pavlova.

Chocolate-Cherry Biscotti

Makes about 36 biscotti

Around the holidays, if I didn't hear my wife say, "Don't forget to make the biscotti" a million times, something would be wrong. It's her absolute favorite. In these biscotti, chocolate and cherry come together in perfect harmony. If you've made biscotti before, you know that they actually get better after a day or two, and also keep for at least a week if stored properly in an airtight container. These are perfect for holiday treats, party gifts, or just to have on hand for your morning coffee. They also have a wonderful appearance and added sweetness when drizzled with rich chocolate ganache. Now you too will be hearing "Don't forget to make the biscotti!"

3 cups all-purpose flour

2 teaspoons baking powder

¼ teaspoon salt

½ cup (1 stick) unsalted butter, at room temperature, plus more for the pan

¾ cup sugar

3 large eggs

2 teaspoons pure almond extract

½ teaspoon pure vanilla extract

½ cup semisweet mini chocolate chips

½ cup candied cherries, roughly chopped

Chocolate Ganache (recipe follows; optional)

Preheat the oven to 350ºF and place the rack in the center. Lightly grease three baking sheets or line them with parchment paper.

In a medium bowl, whisk together the flour, baking powder, and salt; set aside.

In the bowl of a standing mixer fitted with the paddle attachment, cream together the butter and sugar on medium-high speed until light and fluffy, 2 to 3 minutes. Add the eggs, one at a time, beating to combine after each addition, then add the almond and vanilla extracts. Reduce the mixer speed to low, then add the flour mixture and mix until the dough comes together. Stir in the chocolate chips and cherries.

On one prepared baking sheet, form the dough into two 10-inch rounds and flatten them to about 3 inches wide. Bake for 25 minutes, then remove from the oven and let cool slightly, leaving the oven on. Transfer the rounds to a cutting board and use a serrated knife to cut them on an angle into ½-inch slices. Lay the biscotti cut-side down on the remaining prepared baking sheets. Bake for 10 minutes, or until the biscotti start to brown, then flip them and bake for about 5 minutes more. Transfer biscotti to a wire rack set over a baking sheet to cool, then drizzle with chocolate ganache, if desired.

CHOCOLATE GANACHE

. . . .

Makes about 1½ cups

12 ounces semisweet chocolate, chopped into small pieces

1 cup heavy cream

Place the chocolate pieces in a medium bowl. In a small saucepan, bring the heavy cream to a boil over medium-high heat, then pour it over the chocolate and stir until the chocolate has completely melted and the mixture is glossy. Let cool slightly before using.

Chocolate-Espresso Macarons

Chocolate, espresso, and buttercream frosting join forces to make these delicate and delectable macaron cookies. These are one of the two variations I made on The American Baking Competition, *and the theme I used was "Macarons in the Park." I pictured a quaint pastry shop in Paris, across from a beautiful park where you could stroll and enjoy these creations with a special someone. Très romantique! Letting the cookies rest at room temperature after piping, but before baking, is what gives them their classic crunchy exterior and chewy interior textures. Also, a tip for creating the perfect macaron shape is to stencil small circles on parchment paper, flip the paper, and pipe the batter by following the outlines to ensure uniformity.*

4 egg whites, at room temperature

¼ teaspoon cream of tartar

¼ cup superfine sugar

1 teaspoon pure vanilla extract

1 cup almond flour

2 cups confectioners' sugar, sifted

2 tablespoons unsweetened cocoa powder

1 tablespoon espresso powder

Buttercream Frosting (recipe follows), for filling

Preheat the oven to 350°F. Line two rimless baking sheets with parchment paper.

In the bowl of a standing mixer fitted with the whisk attachment, beat together the egg whites and cream of tartar on medium-high speed until soft peaks form, then slowly add the superfine sugar and continue to beat until stiff peaks form. Add the vanilla and mix until blended. Remove the bowl from the mixer and use a rubber spatula to fold in flour, confectioners' sugar, cocoa powder, and espresso powder.

Transfer the mixture to a pastry bag fitted with a ½-inch plain tip. Pipe it into 1½-inch mounds onto the prepared baking sheets, about 1 inch apart. Bang the sheets against the counter to remove air bubbles, then smooth any pointy tips with an offset spatula. Let stand at room temperature for 35 to 45 minutes.

Bake until the tops and bottoms are firm, about 15 minutes. Remove from the oven and transfer to wire racks to cool completely. Spread 1 teaspoon of buttercream frosting on the flat side of one macaron, then sandwich together with the flat side of another macaron. Repeat until you have filled all the macarons.

BUTTERCREAM FROSTING

Makes about 2 cups

½ cup (1 stick) unsalted butter, at room temperature

3¾ cups confectioners' sugar

3 to 4 teaspoons whole milk

1 teaspoon pure vanilla extract

In the bowl of a standing mixer fitted with the paddle attachment, cream together the butter and sugar on low speed. Once combined, raise the mixer speed to medium and continue to beat until light and fluffy, 2 to 3 minutes more. Add 3 teaspoons of the milk and continue to mix for another minute. Add the remaining 1 teaspoon milk, if necessary, to achieve the desired consistency, and stir in the vanilla.

Chocolate Macarons

Anyone who visits Paris and walks into any pastry shop will see rows of these eye-popping, colorful French macarons. The combinations of flavors and fillings appear endless, and the precise beauty of them is really amazing. They have become increasingly popular in pastry shops here in the States as well, and are a great treat to know how to make. Once you have the technique nailed down, get creative and test different flavors and fillings, and pretend you're making macarons for your own little shop in France. I know I do!

4 egg whites, at room temperature

¼ teaspoon cream of tartar

¼ cup superfine sugar

1 teaspoon pure vanilla extract

1 cup almond flour

2 cups confectioners' sugar, sifted

3 tablespoons unsweetened cocoa powder

Almond-Chocolate Ganache (recipe follows)

Preheat the oven to 350°F. Line two rimless baking sheets with parchment paper.

In the bowl of a standing mixer fitted with the whisk attachment, beat together the egg whites and cream of tartar on medium-high speed until soft peaks form, then slowly add the superfine sugar and continue to beat until stiff peaks form. Add the vanilla and mix until blended. Remove the bowl from the mixer and use a rubber spatula to fold in almond flour, confectioners' sugar, and cocoa powder.

Transfer the mixture to a pastry bag fitted with a ½-inch plain tip. Pipe it into 1½-inch mounds onto the prepared baking sheets, about 1 inch apart. Bang the sheets against the counter to remove air bubbles, then smooth any pointy tips with an offset spatula. Let stand at room temperature for 35 to 45 minutes.

Bake until the tops and bottoms are firm, about 15 minutes. Remove from the oven and transfer to wire racks to cool completely. Spread 1 teaspoon of almond-chocolate ganache on the flat side of one macaron, then sandwich it together with the flat side of another macaron. Repeat until you have filled all the macarons.

ALMOND-CHOCOLATE GANACHE
. . . .

Makes about ¾ cup

6 ounces good-quality bittersweet (60 to 64% cacao) chocolate, such as Ghirardelli, finely chopped

2 tablespoons unsalted butter, at room temperature

½ cup heavy cream

1 teaspoon almond extract

Place the chocolate in a medium bowl and set aside. In a small saucepan, heat the butter and cream until small bubbles form around the sides of the pan and the butter has melted completely. Pour the hot cream mixture over the chocolate and stir until the chocolate has melted completely. Stir in the almond extract. Let cool slightly before using.

Hazelnut Macarons

I must admit . . . I'm slightly obsessed with French pastries, especially the beautiful and divine macaron. In this version, hazelnuts lend the most amazing nutty flavor and Nutella takes them to an even higher level of deliciousness. It's important to grind the hazelnuts into a very fine powder so that the texture of the cookie is smooth. To remove the skins of the hazelnuts, toast the nuts until fragrant and lightly browned and then rub them between a towel. The skins should easily come off. As an alternative, buy them without skins and toast them until lightly golden, then finely grind them. Remember to let the cookie batter rest on the baking sheet for 35 to 45 minutes before baking—it's a step that will truly make a difference in the end.

4 egg whites, at room temperature

¼ teaspoon cream of tartar

¼ cup superfine sugar

1 teaspoon pure vanilla extract

¼ teaspoon pure almond extract

1 cup hazelnuts, toasted, skins removed, very finely ground

2 cups confectioners' sugar, sifted

½ cup Nutella

Preheat the oven to 350ºF. Line two rimless baking sheets with parchment paper.

In the bowl of a standing mixer fitted with the whisk attachment, beat together the egg whites and cream of tartar on medium-high speed until soft peaks form, then slowly add the superfine sugar and continue to beat until stiff peaks form. Add the vanilla and almond extracts and mix until blended. Remove the bowl from the mixer and use a rubber spatula to fold in the ground hazelnuts and confectioners' sugar until blended.

Transfer the mixture to a pastry bag fitted with a ½-inch plain tip. Pipe it in 1½-inch mounds onto the prepared baking sheets, about 1 inch apart. Bang the sheets against the counter to remove air bubbles, then smooth any pointy tips with an offset spatula. Let stand at room temperature for 35 to 45 minutes.

Bake until the tops and bottoms are firm, about 15 minutes. Remove from the oven and transfer to wire racks to cool completely. Spread 1 teaspoon of Nutella on the flat side of one macaron, then sandwich it together with the flat side of a second macaron. Repeat until you have filled all the macarons.

Double Chocolate Brownies

Makes 8 brownies

Moist and chewy, these super-rich brownies pack a double chocolate punch. You will be hard-pressed to find someone who doesn't want to gobble these up immediately. Just ask my kids! This is such a great recipe to have on hand when you need a showstopping dessert but don't have a ton of time. I like to make these and use round cookie cutters to cut out circles, then layer them with vanilla ice cream, sometimes three stacks high, and freeze. Then when I throw a dinner party, I take them out of the freezer and top them with chocolate sauce and fresh whipped cream. Makes a perfect do-ahead dessert that is elegant, easy, and delicious.

½ cup (1 stick) unsalted butter, plus more for the pan

2 ounces of quality unsweetened chocolate, such as Ghirardelli, chopped

1 teaspoon pure vanilla extract

¾ cup all-purpose flour

¼ teaspoon baking powder

2 large eggs

1 cup sugar

½ cup quality semisweet chocolate chips, such as Ghirardelli

¾ cup chopped nuts (optional)

Preheat the oven to 350ºF. Lightly grease an 11 x 7-inch pan.

In the top of a double boiler over barely simmering water, melt the butter and chocolate together. Stir until completely smooth, remove from the heat, and stir in the vanilla. Set aside to cool.

In a medium bowl, sift together the flour and baking powder three times; set aside.

In the bowl of a standing mixer fitted with the whisk attachment, or in a bowl using a hand mixer, beat the eggs until fluffy, then add the sugar and beat well until pale yellow. Use a wooden spoon or rubber spatula to stir in the melted chocolate mixture and the flour until completely combined, then fold in the chocolate chips. Add nuts, if using. Spread the batter in the prepared pan and bake for 25 to 30 minutes, or until a toothpick inserted into the center comes out clean. Let cool in the pan, then cut into 8 squares and serve.

Gingersnaps

I love the combination of warm spices that give these gingersnaps so much depth of flavor and aroma. There is nothing like the smell of these cookies baking to get everyone in the mood for celebration and good times together. Even though I typically make these during the holidays, this recipe is incredibly easy and quick to assemble, so I like to keep them in mind as a simple treat to whip up any time of year.

2 cups all-purpose flour

2 teaspoons baking soda

½ teaspoon ground cloves

½ teaspoon ground ginger

1 teaspoon ground cinnamon

½ teaspoon salt

¾ cup (1½ sticks) unsalted butter, melted

1½ cups sugar

¼ cup molasses

1 large egg

Preheat the oven to 350°F. Line two baking sheets with parchment paper.

In a small bowl, sift together the flour, baking soda, cloves, ginger, cinnamon, and salt.

In a medium bowl, whisk together the melted butter, 1 cup of the sugar, the molasses, and the egg. Add the dry ingredients and stir until completely combined.

Place the remaining ½ cup sugar on a plate. Form the dough into 1-inch balls, rolling them between your palms to make them smooth. Roll the balls in the sugar to coat and place them 2 inches apart on the prepared baking sheets. Bake for 8 to 10 minutes, then transfer to wire racks to cool.

Old-Fashioned Raisin Cookies

Makes 48 cookies

I grew up in a house that was always filled with fresh homemade cookies and cakes. My mom had a reputation as the best baker in our neighborhood and all the other kids would conveniently drop by when she had fresh-baked sweets after school. These cakey and soft old-fashioned raisin cookies were always the favorite—she would even make a double batch because they would disappear too fast. My siblings and I got to pick the "cookie of the week" that she would make, and I always asked for these. Even if she made one of my sibling's choices she would sneak in a batch of these for me. I guess it sometimes pays to be the youngest of the brood!

3 cups all-purpose flour

1 teaspoon baking soda

1 teaspoon salt

1 teaspoon freshly grated nutmeg

1 teaspoon ground cinnamon

1 cup vegetable shortening

2 cups packed light brown sugar

2 large eggs

½ cup brewed coffee, cooled to room temperature

1 cup raisins

Preheat the oven to 350°F and place the rack in the center.

In a medium bowl, whisk together the flour, baking soda, salt, nutmeg, and cinnamon. Set aside.

In the bowl of a standing mixer fitted with the paddle attachment, beat together the shortening and sugar on medium-high speed until light and fluffy, 2 to 3 minutes. Add the eggs one at a time, blending completely after each addition and scraping down the bowl as necessary with a rubber spatula. Mix in the cold coffee. Reduce the mixer speed to low, add the flour mixture, and mix until completely combined. Remove the bowl from the mixer and use a rubber spatula to fold in the raisins.

Using a 2-ounce ice cream scoop or heaping tablespoon, drop dough onto baking sheets, leaving 2 inches between each cookie. Bake until the cookies are lightly golden with a soft texture, 10 to 12 minutes. Let cool slightly on pans, then move to wire racks or directly on counter to cool completely.

Orange Oatmeal Chews

Makes about 2 dozen

There's something about oatmeal cookies . . . I always feel like I'm doing something good for myself when I eat them. Knowing that the key ingredient, oatmeal, is super healthy and considered a "power food," I feel justified to have these on hand any time I want a sugar treat without feeling guilty. These chewy cookies are packed with so much flavor, you will fall in love after the first bite. Toasted oatmeal and walnuts together with fresh orange zest make for a fantastic combination and delicious version of the classic oatmeal cookie.

1 cup old-fashioned rolled oats

¾ cup all-purpose flour

1 teaspoon salt

½ teaspoon baking soda

½ cup granulated sugar

½ cup packed light brown sugar

½ cup (1 stick) unsalted butter, at room temperature

1 large egg

1 teaspoon pure vanilla extract

2 tablespoons grated orange zest

½ cup chopped walnuts

Preheat the oven to 350ºF. On a small baking sheet, toast the oats in the oven for about 5 minutes, stirring frequently to avoid burning. Transfer the oats to a medium bowl (leaving the oven on), add the flour, salt, and baking soda, and whisk to combine.

In the bowl of a standing mixer fitted with the paddle attachment, cream together both sugars and the butter on medium-high speed until light and fluffy, 2 to 3 minutes. Add the egg and beat until completely combined, then mix in vanilla and orange zest. Reduce the mixer speed to low, add the oat mixture, and mix until completely combined. Remove the bowl from the mixer and stir or fold in the walnuts.

Line two baking sheets with parchment paper and drop heaping teaspoons of the dough onto the prepared baking sheets. Bake for 10 to 12 minutes, then transfer to a wire rack to cool.

Spritz Cookies

These delicate and decorative cookies are perfect for the holidays. Sprinkle with red, green, or silver sanding sugar for added glitz, or drizzle with a citrus, chocolate, or vanilla glaze. I usually make a big batch and give them away as gifts, but I always make sure to keep some in the house to have with my morning coffee or afternoon tea. Just remember you will need a cookie press, which you can buy at most baking stores. For a chocolate variation of the spritz, follow the same basic recipe but add 1½ squares of unsweetened baking chocolate melted into the butter mixture.

1 cup (2 sticks) unsalted butter, at room temperature

¾ cup sugar

3 large egg yolks

½ teaspoon pure almond extract

½ teaspoon pure vanilla extract

2½ cups all-purpose flour, sifted

Sanding sugar, for sprinkling (optional)

Preheat the oven to 400°F.

In the bowl of a standing mixer fitted with the paddle attachment, cream together the butter and sugar on medium-high speed until light and fluffy, about 2 minutes. Add the egg yolks and mix until completely combined, then add the almond and vanilla extracts. Reduce the mixer speed to low and gradually mix in the flour until the dough comes together. Refrigerate for 1 hour.

Fill a cookie press with dough and fit with a disc to make the shape you desire. Press the dough directly onto an ungreased baking sheet, leaving 1½ inches between each cookie, and sprinkle with sanding sugar (if using). Bake until golden, 8 to 10 minutes, then transfer to wire racks to cool.

Pumpkin Bars

Makes 12 to 15 bars

Every fall, we have a big neighborhood party to celebrate the season and everyone brings food and treats for a festive outdoor potluck. These pumpkin bars get gobbled up so fast, they are always the first to go! I like to use canned pumpkin, just plain pumpkin without spices added, but feel free to use fresh pumpkin, cooked and pureed, instead. I like to add warm spices such as cinnamon and nutmeg, which provide a wonderful aroma and taste, and the cream cheese frosting gives the bars an added subtle sweetness. Feel free to double this frosting, as I like a thick layer on top! These pumpkin bars would be a great addition to any Thanksgiving dessert spread, Halloween celebration, or casual party.

Nonstick cooking spray or vegetable oil, for the pan

2 cups all-purpose flour

2 cups sugar

½ teaspoon salt

2 teaspoons baking soda

2 teaspoons baking powder

2 teaspoons ground cinnamon

½ teaspoon freshly grated nutmeg

4 large eggs

1 cup vegetable oil

2 cups pure pumpkin puree

Cream Cheese Frosting (recipe follows)

½ cup pecans, toasted and roughly chopped (optional)

Preheat the oven to 350ºF. Spray a 9 x 13-inch baking pan with nonstick cooking spray or brush with vegetable oil. Set aside.

In a medium bowl, whisk together the flour, sugar, salt, baking soda, baking powder, cinnamon, and nutmeg until combined. In a separate bowl, whisk together the eggs, oil, and pumpkin puree until well blended. Add the egg mixture to the flour mixture and stir until completely combined.

Pour the batter into the prepared baking pan and bake for about 35 to 40 minutes, or until a toothpick inserted into the center comes out clean. Let cool in the pan. Frost the top of the cake with cream cheese frosting and sprinkle with toasted, chopped walnuts, if desired. I love to double this recipe and make a super thick layer of frosting. Cut into bars and serve.

CREAM CHEESE FROSTING

Makes about 2 cups

3 ounces cream cheese, at room temperature

6 tablespoons (¾ stick) unsalted butter, at room temperature

1 teaspoon heavy cream, plus more as needed

1 teaspoon pure vanilla extract

1¾ cups confectioners' sugar

In the bowl of a standing mixer fitted with the paddle attachment, beat together the cream cheese and butter on medium speed until light and fluffy, about 2 minutes. Reduce the mixer speed to low, add the heavy cream, vanilla, and sugar, and continue to mix until smooth and well combined. Add more heavy cream, 1 teaspoon at a time, if needed to achieve the desired consistency.

Salted Peanut Cookies

Makes about 48 cookies

I am crazy for peanuts, so this cookie recipe is one of my personal favorites. Salty and sweet with a touch of crunch, I find these completely addicting. I've added cornflakes and oatmeal to the recipe for texture and also to balance the salt from the peanuts and sweetness from the sugars. You can substitute cashews or almonds for the peanuts if you prefer, or use a combination of all three.

2 cups all-purpose flour

1 teaspoon baking soda

1 cup cornflakes

2 cups old-fashioned rolled oats

1 cup salted peanuts

1 cup (2 sticks) unsalted butter, at room temperature

1 cup granulated sugar

1 cup packed light brown sugar

2 large eggs

½ teaspoon pure vanilla extract

Preheat the oven to 400°F. Line two baking sheets with parchment paper.

In a large bowl, stir together the flour, baking soda, cornflakes, oats, and peanuts; set aside.

In the bowl of a standing mixer fitted with the paddle attachment, cream together the butter and both sugars on medium-high speed until light and fluffy, about 2 minutes. Add the eggs one at a time, blending completely after each addition and scraping down the bowl as necessary with a rubber spatula. Add the vanilla, then reduce the mixer speed to low, add the cornflake mixture, and mix until just combined.

Use a heaping teaspoon to drop dough onto the prepared baking sheets, leaving about 2 inches between each cookie. Bake for 10 to 12 minutes, until golden. Let cool for 5 minutes on baking sheets, then transfer to a wire rack and let cool.

Cakes

Introduction to Cakes

Cakes are a universal symbol of celebration. They come in so many shapes, sizes, and colors and all have unique qualities that make them special. They show up when there is a birthday, baby shower, promotion, wedding . . . really any occasion that is cause for having a party or making someone feel special. We all have our favorites too, and each cake in this book has special meaning for me and for the most important people in my life. My daughter loves the Classic Yellow Cake with Vanilla Buttercream Frosting (page 155) and we have the best time going crazy with inventive and over-the-top decorations for her birthday every year. My mother-in-law is all about the Cheesecake with Lemon Curd Topping (page 148) so I make sure I have this made any time she visits. And for me, the Berry Trifle Cake (page 134) is my absolute favorite; in fact I make it for my own birthday every year!

In my opinion, the most satisfying thing about making cakes is putting flair on the decorations and toppings; I love to tap into my creative side and let the rules go. Anything from sugar-coated flowers to candied citrus, fresh berries, or shaved chocolate. And of course, lots of delicious frosting and toppings take these cakes to a wonderfully decadent place.

The trick to making a light, moist cake is to be mindful of a few simple techniques:

- First, really take the time to cream the butter and sugar until light and fluffy. This step is important for incorporating air into the batter, which gives your cakes more volume.

- Add the eggs one at a time and mix until completely combined before adding the next. Use a rubber spatula to scrape down the sides of the bowl throughout the process to evenly distribute all the ingredients.

- Add the flour and liquid in three or four additions, alternating between flour and liquid, and beginning and ending with the flour. If you add everything at once, the batter will lose air and the result will be flat cakes. When adding flour to the cake batter, reduce the mixer speed to low and be careful not to overmix. Beating flour releases its gluten, and when overbeaten, flour will become tough, resulting in a less light and airy texture in your final product.

- Make sure your oven is preheated to the proper temperature with the rack set in the middle, and that you rotate the pans halfway through the baking time.

- Finally, after removing the baked cakes from your pans, allow them time to cool before you attempt to frost or decorate them.

Now on to the frosting! Turntable cake stands are great because they rotate and make it so much easier to work evenly on all sides. Of course if you do not have a turntable, a large plate or platter will work as well. Place strips of waxed or parchment paper under the edges of the bottom of the cake so that, once the cake is frosted, all you need to do is pull the strips out and you have a clean surface. It's also a great idea to use an offset spatula to frost your cake as it's easier to control the smoothing and design-focused strokes.

To perfectly frost a cake, follow these simple steps:

1. Use a brush to lightly whisk away some of the loose cake crumbs on the top and sides.

2. Take about one third of the frosting, thin it out with a tiny bit of water, then cover the cake with a very thin layer of frosting. Applying this "crumb coat" will ultimately help adhere all the crumbs to the cake and make for a smoother finish once you apply the final frosting layers. It is important to let the crumb coat dry completely before you proceed with frosting the rest of the cake.

3. Place about 1 cup of frosting in the center on top of the cake and work the frosting to the outer edges, then work the frosting from the top of the cake down the sides, adding more frosting as needed. Hold the spatula upright and turn the cake stand or plate to frost all of the sides, making smooth strokes as you rotate.

Now that you have the tools and techniques fresh in your mind, I think we are ready to make some fantastic cakes! The recipes in this chapter are meant to be made with love and shared to bring joy into people's lives. Enjoy the process, have fun, and celebrate!

Berry Trifle Cake

Serves 8

I'm one of those crazy people who makes their own birthday cake. Although it may sound strange, I want to make sure it's going to be exactly what I want on my big day. This trifle cake is my long-standing birthday choice and as my family will attest, it makes a grand statement every year! To make a big fanfare of the presentation, use sparkler candles and lots of mixed berries for garnish.

1 cup (2 sticks) unsalted butter, at room temperature, plus more for the pan

3 cups cake flour, plus more for the pan

2 teaspoons baking powder

½ teaspoon salt

2 cups sugar

4 large eggs

1 teaspoon pure vanilla extract

½ teaspoon berry extract

¾ cup whole milk

1 box Berry Jell-O gelatin mix

2 ounces Chambord (optional)

Vanilla Pudding (recipe follows, page 136)

Whipped Cream (page 15)

Mixed fresh berries, such as strawberries, blueberries, raspberries, and blackberries, for garnish

Preheat the oven to 350°F and place the rack in the center. Butter and lightly flour a 9 x 13-inch baking pan.

In a medium bowl, sift together the cake flour, baking powder, and salt; set aside.

In the bowl of a standing mixer fitted with the paddle attachment, beat the butter on medium speed. Add the sugar and beat until light and fluffy, 2 to 3 minutes. Add the eggs one at a time, blending completely after each addition and scraping down the bowl as necessary with a rubber spatula. Add the vanilla and berry extracts, then reduce the mixer speed to low. Add the flour mixture and the milk alternately in three additions, beginning and ending with the flour.

Pour the batter into the prepared pan and bake for 20 to 25 minutes, or until a toothpick or cake tester inserted into the center comes out clean.

In a medium bowl, combine the gelatin mix with 2 cups hot water and add Chambord, if using. Let cake cool completely in pan, and leave cake in pan as you begin to decorate. Use a toothpick to prick holes into the top of the cake and then pour the gelatin mixture completely over it. Top the cake with vanilla pudding, then whipped cream. Decorate with mixed berries and serve.

VANILLA PUDDING

2 cups whole milk

1 cup heavy cream

¾ cup sugar

3 tablespoons cornstarch

$\frac{1}{8}$ teaspoon salt

3 large egg yolks

2 teaspoons pure vanilla extract

1 tablespoon unsalted butter, cut into pieces

In a small saucepan, combine the milk, cream, sugar, cornstarch, and salt and whisk to combine. Bring to a simmer over medium-high heat and cook, whisking continuously, until the sugar has dissolved and the mixture starts to thicken, 3 to 4 minutes. Remove from the heat.

In a medium bowl, whisk the eggs until pale and frothy, about 3 minutes. While whisking continuously, slowly add about ½ cup of the hot milk mixture to the eggs, then whisk the egg mixture back into the hot milk mixture and return to medium-low heat. Cook, whisking continuously, for 1 minute. Bring to a simmer, stirring continuously with a wooden spoon, and cook until thickened, about 2 minutes. Remove from the heat and stir in the vanilla and butter, stirring until the butter has melted completely and the mixture is combined. Transfer to a nonreactive bowl, cover with plastic wrap, and let cool for at least 2 hours. The pudding can be made ahead of time and chilled for up to 4 hours before using.

Blueberry Buckle

Serves 6 to 8

Blueberry buckle is a classic streusel cake topped with sweet blueberries and a spiced crumble that is simply delicious. Enjoy eating it as a coffee cake for breakfast or as a cake for dessert. Either way, this is a big crowd-pleaser!

Butter, melted, for the pans

1 pint fresh blueberries

2 teaspoons fresh lemon juice

$\frac{1}{3}$ cup plus $\frac{1}{2}$ cup sugar

$2\frac{1}{3}$ cups all-purpose flour

$\frac{1}{2}$ teaspoon ground cinnamon

$\frac{1}{2}$ teaspoon freshly grated nutmeg

4 tablespoons ($\frac{1}{2}$ stick) unsalted butter, cut into pieces and kept cold, plus $\frac{1}{2}$ cup (1 stick) unsalted butter, at room temperature

$\frac{1}{2}$ teaspoon salt

$2\frac{1}{2}$ teaspoons baking powder

1 large egg

$\frac{1}{2}$ cup plus 2 tablespoons whole milk

Preheat the oven to 350°F. Line a 9 x 9-inch pan with parchment paper, then brush the paper and the sides of the pan with butter.

In a small bowl, mix the blueberries with the lemon juice; set aside. In another bowl, stir together $\frac{1}{3}$ cup of the sugar, $\frac{1}{3}$ cup of the flour, the cinnamon, and the nutmeg. Using a pastry blender or fork, cut the 4 tablespoons cold butter into the mixture until it resembles coarse crumbs. Refrigerate until ready to use.

In a medium bowl, sift together the remaining 2 cups flour, the salt, and the baking powder and set aside.

In the bowl of a standing mixer fitted with the paddle attachment, cream together the remaining ½ cup room temperature butter and ½ cup sugar on medium-high speed until light and fluffy, about 2 minutes. Add the egg and beat until completely combined. Reduce the mixer speed to low and add the flour mixture and milk alternately in three additions, beginning and ending with the flour.

Pour the batter into the prepared pan, spreading it a little higher toward the edges. Spoon the berries evenly over the batter, then sprinkle with the cinnamon and sugar crumble mixture.

Bake for 50 to 60 minutes, or until a toothpick or cake tester inserted into the center comes out clean. Remove from the oven and let cool in the pan for 8 to 10 minutes, then lift the cake out of the pan using the edges of the parchment paper. Alternatively, invert the cake onto a large plate, remove the parchment paper, then reinvert the cake and let cool slightly. Serve warm.

Blueberry Meringue Cloud Cake

These meringue cakes are appropriately named as they are light, airy, and take your taste buds to the clouds! They're surprisingly easy to make, but the results are impressive and delicious. Here are three simple but important tips to keep in mind:

1. Measure and mark your 9-inch circles on parchment before piping.

2. Make sure the blueberries are mashed well so that they easily pipe through a ½-inch pastry tip, and . . .

3. When piping, hold the tip slightly away from the surface to ensure a smooth and "cloudlike" appearance.

2 cups fresh blueberries, plus more for garnish

2 tablespoons light corn syrup

6 large egg whites, at room temperature

⅛ teaspoon cream of tartar

Pinch of salt

½ cup superfine sugar

¼ teaspoon plus ½ teaspoon pure vanilla extract

2 cups heavy cream

½ cup confectioners' sugar

Fresh mint sprigs, for garnish

Preheat the oven to 300°F. Line two baking sheets with parchment paper.

In a small bowl, combine the blueberries with the corn syrup and gently stir to coat. Place the berries on an unlined rimmed baking sheet and bake for about 1 hour, until the berries are soft and completely cooked through. Let cool slightly on the baking sheet, then transfer to a bowl and use a fork or the back of a spoon to mash. Set aside to cool.

In the bowl of a standing mixer fitted with the whisk attachment, beat together the egg whites, cream of tartar, and salt on medium-high speed until soft peaks form. Slowly add the superfine sugar and beat until the mixture is thick and holds stiff peaks. Add ¼ teaspoon of the vanilla and beat until combined. Remove the bowl from the mixer and use a rubber spatula to gently fold in the mashed blueberries.

Transfer the meringue filling to a pastry bag fitted with a ½-inch plain tip. Pipe the meringue, starting in the middle, in a circular motion to make a 9-inch circle. Repeat three more times to make a total of four 9-inch circles. Bake the meringues until crisp, 50 to 60 minutes. Remove from the oven and let cool on the baking sheets on wire racks.

In a large bowl or in the bowl of a standing mixer fitted with the whisk attachment, whisk the heavy cream, gradually adding the confectioners' sugar and remaining ½ teaspoon vanilla, until soft peaks form. Cover and chill the whipped cream until ready to serve.

To assemble, lay one meringue disc on a plate and top with 1 cup of the whipped cream. Repeat, layering the meringue discs and whipped cream, until you have used all four discs. Top the stack with whipped cream in the center. Garnish with fresh blueberries and fresh mint.

Carrot Cake with Maple-Mascarpone Frosting

Makes one 8-inch double-layer cake

Carrot cake is always a huge crowd-pleaser and one of my most requested desserts. The process is very easy, with no special electrical equipment or mixing machines needed! The carrots lend texture and a subtle sweetness to the cake that matches well with the warm spices and maple-mascarpone frosting. The result is a moist, perfectly dense, and absolutely delicious cake.

Nonstick cooking spray or butter, for the pans

All-purpose flour, for the pans

2 cups cake flour

2 teaspoons baking soda

2 teaspoons baking powder

1 teaspoon ground cinnamon

½ teaspoon freshly grated nutmeg

¼ teaspoon ground cloves

Pinch of salt

1¾ cups sugar

1¼ cups canola oil

1 teaspoon pure vanilla extract

4 large eggs

3 cups grated carrots (grated on the medium holes of a box grater)

Maple-Mascarpone Frosting (recipe follows)

1 cup roughly chopped walnuts (optional)

Preheat the oven to 350°F. Grease the bottom and sides of two 8-inch round cake pans with nonstick cooking spray or butter, then line the pans with 8-inch rounds of parchment paper cut to fit. Grease the parchment paper, and then dust the pans with all-purpose flour, tapping out any excess.

In a medium bowl, sift together the cake flour, baking soda, baking powder, cinnamon, nutmeg, cloves, and salt. Set aside.

In a large bowl, whisk together the sugar, oil, and vanilla. Beat in the eggs one at a time until completely incorporated. Mix in the dry ingredients, then fold in the carrots.

Divide the batter evenly between the prepared pans and bake for about 45 minutes, or until a toothpick or cake tester inserted into the center of the cake comes out clean. Let cool in the pans on wire racks for 10 minutes. Invert the cakes onto the racks, remove the parchment, then immediately reinvert and let cool completely.

Using a serrated knife, gently trim the tops of the cakes to make them level. Place the first cake layer on a cake plate and frost the top with about 1 cup of the maple mascarpone frosting. Place the second layer on top, then frost the entire cake with the remaining frosting. Garnish with chopped walnuts, if desired, and slice to serve.

MAPLE-MASCARPONE FROSTING

2 (8-ounce) packages cream cheese, at room temperature

8 ounces mascarpone cheese

1 pound confectioners' sugar (about 3¾ cups)

2 teaspoons pure vanilla extract

¼ cup pure maple syrup

In the bowl of a standing mixer fitted with the paddle attachment, beat together the cream cheese and mascarpone on medium speed until light and fluffy, 1 to 2 minutes. Slowly add the sugar, then add the vanilla and maple syrup and continue to beat until completely combined. Use immediately or keep refrigerated for up to 24 hours.

Cheesecake with Caramel-Apple Topping

Makes one 9-inch cheesecake

During the process of trying out for a spot on The American Baking Competition, *I was asked to make my favorite dessert and present it to the casting committee. I chose this cheesecake and am happy to say, they LOVED it! The mix of cream cheese with mascarpone and sour cream lends to a smooth, tangy, and rich texture and taste. Paired with the decadent caramel-apple topping and caramel sauce, this cake is simply irresistible.*

7 tablespoons unsalted butter, cut into pieces, at room temperature

1¼ cups sugar

1 large egg yolk

1¼ cups all-purpose flour

2 ¼ ounces crushed almonds

3 (8-ounce) packages cream cheese, at room temperature

8 ounces mascarpone cheese, at room temperature

¼ cup sour cream, at room temperature

2 large eggs

1 vanilla bean, split and seeds scraped

1 teaspoon pure vanilla extract

Caramel-Apple Topping (recipe follows, page 146)

Caramel Sauce (recipe follows, page 147)

Whipped Cream (page 15)

In a medium bowl, use a wooden spoon or rubber spatula to combine the butter and ¼ cup of the sugar into a paste. Add the egg yolk and blend thoroughly. Add the flour and crushed almonds, then use your fingers to blend until the mixture resembles fine crumbs and holds together when pinched. Press the mixture firmly into the bottom and up the sides of a 9-inch springform pan, then refrigerate for 30 minutes.

Preheat the oven to 400°F.

Remove the shortbread crust from the refrigerator and prick the bottom all over with a fork. Line the dough with parchment paper or foil and fill with pie weights. Blind bake the crust for 10 to 12 minutes, then remove pie weights and foil or parchment and bake for 5 minutes more, or until golden. Reduce the oven temperature to 325°F. Set the crust aside to cool completely on a wire rack, then wrap the outside of the springform pan in foil and set it in a larger pan, such as a roasting pan; set aside.

In the bowl of a standing mixer fitted with the paddle attachment, beat together the cream cheese, mascarpone, and sour cream until well blended. Slowly add the remaining 1 cup sugar and beat until light and fluffy, about 2 minutes. Use a rubber spatula to scrape down the sides of the bowl, then beat in the eggs, one at a time, until completely incorporated. Add the vanilla seeds and vanilla extract and continue to beat until combined.

Pour the mixture into the prepared crust. Fill the larger pan with hot water so it comes halfway up the sides of the springform pan. Bake for about 1 hour, until the cheesecake is set but has a slight jiggle in the middle. Remove the cheesecake from the water bath, let cool, and then remove the foil and refrigerate in the springform pan until set and chilled, 2 hours or up to overnight.

When ready to serve, take the cheesecake out of the refrigerator and remove the outer ring from the springform pan. Spoon the caramel-apple topping over the cake, then drizzle with caramel sauce. Slice and serve with fresh whipped cream.

CARAMEL-APPLE TOPPING

. . . .

½ cup (1 stick) unsalted butter

¼ cup granulated sugar

¼ cup packed light brown sugar

4 to 5 Granny Smith apples, peeled, cored, and cut into 1½-inch wedges

½ teaspoon apple cider vinegar

½ teaspoon ground cinnamon

½ teaspoon freshly grated nutmeg

In a large sauté pan, melt the butter and both sugars together over medium-low heat. Add the apples, vinegar, cinnamon, and nutmeg and cook, stirring occasionally, until the apples are tender and caramelized, about 15 minutes. Set aside to cool.

CARAMEL SAUCE

Makes 1½ cups

1 cup packed light brown sugar

½ cup (1 stick) unsalted butter

½ teaspoon pure vanilla extract

¼ cup heavy cream

¼ cup honey

Pinch of salt

In a medium saucepan, combine the sugar, butter, vanilla, heavy cream, honey, and salt. Bring to a boil over medium heat. Cook for about 2 minutes, then remove from the heat. Let cool slightly before using.

Cheesecake with Lemon Curd Topping

Makes one 9-inch cheesecake

I'm what you might call a cheesecake fanatic, and I love to come up with ideas for toppings that match the quality of such a delicious cake. This version with lemon curd has the perfect balance in flavors between tart, sweet, lemony, and tangy. I like to "gild the lily" on this stand-alone beauty by garnishing it with fresh whipped cream and candied lemons. A great thing to note about this recipe is that lemon curd can be made ahead of time and stored in the refrigerator for up to two weeks, making day-of assembly a breeze.

7 tablespoons unsalted butter, cut into pieces, at room temperature

1¼ cups sugar

1 large egg yolk

1¼ cups all-purpose flour

2 tablespoons grated lemon zest

1 tablespoon fresh lemon juice

3 (8-ounce) packages cream cheese, at room temperature

8 ounces mascarpone cheese, at room temperature

¼ cup sour cream, at room temperature

2 large eggs

1 vanilla bean, split and seeds scraped

1 teaspoon pure vanilla extract

Lemon Curd (recipe follows)

Candied Lemons (recipe follows)

Whipped Cream (page 15)

In a medium bowl, use a wooden spoon or rubber spatula to combine the butter and ¼ cup of the sugar into a paste. Add the egg yolk and mix thoroughly. Add the flour, lemon zest, and lemon juice. Blend until the mixture resembles fine crumbs and holds together when pinched. Press the mixture firmly into the bottom and up the sides of a 9-inch springform pan, then refrigerate for 30 minutes.

Preheat the oven to 400°F. Remove the shortbread crust from the refrigerator and prick the bottom all over with a fork. Line the dough with parchment paper or foil and fill it with pie weights. Blind bake the crust for 10 to 12 minutes, then remove the pie weights and foil or parchment and bake for 5 minutes more, or until golden. Reduce the oven temperature to 325°F. Set the crust aside to cool completely on a wire rack, then wrap the outside of the springform pan in foil and place it in a larger pan, such as a roasting pan; set aside.

In the bowl of a standing mixer fitted with the paddle attachment, beat together the cream cheese, mascarpone, and sour cream until well blended. Slowly add the remaining 1 cup sugar and beat until light and fluffy, about 2 minutes. Use a rubber spatula to scrape down the sides of the bowl, then beat in the eggs, one at a time, until completely incorporated. Add the vanilla seeds and vanilla extract and continue to beat until combined.

Pour the mixture into the crust. Fill the larger pan with hot water so it comes halfway up the sides of the springform pan. Bake for about 1 hour, until the cheesecake is set but has a slight jiggle in the middle. Remove the cheesecake from the water bath, let cool, and then remove the foil and refrigerate in the springform pan until set and chilled, 2 hours or up to overnight.

When ready to serve, take the cheesecake out of the refrigerator and remove the outer ring from the springform pan. Take 1 cup of the lemon curd and spread it over the cheesecake. Decorate with candied lemons and fresh whipped cream. Slice to serve.

LEMON CURD

Makes about 2 cups

½ cup (1 stick) unsalted butter, at room temperature

1¾ cups sugar

4 large eggs

Zest of 2 lemons

1 cup fresh lemon juice

Pinch of salt

In the bowl of a standing mixer fitted with the paddle attachment, cream together the butter and sugar on medium-high speed until light and fluffy, about 2 minutes. Scrape down the sides of the bowl, then beat in the eggs, one at a time, until completely incorporated. Add the lemon zest, lemon juice, and salt, then continue to beat until combined. Pour the mixture into a medium saucepan and cook over medium heat, whisking continuously, until thickened, 10 to 12 minutes.

Remove from the heat and transfer the lemon curd to a bowl. Cover with plastic wrap, pressing the plastic directly against the curd to prevent a skin from forming. Let cool to room temperature, then refrigerate until well chilled, at least 3 hours. The lemon curd will keep in the refrigerator for up to 2 weeks.

CANDIED LEMONS

3 small lemons

1¼ cups sugar

¼ cup fresh lemon juice

Cut the lemons crosswise into slices about ⅛ inch thick and remove any seeds. In a large skillet, stir together the sugar, lemon juice, and about 2 cups water and cook over medium heat until the sugar has dissolved. Add the lemon slices and cook, turning occasionally, for about 15 minutes or until they become translucent. Remove from the heat and use tongs to transfer to a baking sheet lined with waxed paper. Let cool completely, and then refrigerate for at least 3 hours, or until ready to use.

Chocolate Layer Cake with Chocolate Buttercream Frosting

Makes one 8-inch double-layer cake

This divine cake is every chocolate lover's dream come true! My secret to the rich, moist texture and dense crumb is the last-minute addition of boiling water to the batter. This chocolate cake with velvety rich chocolate buttercream frosting is completely irresistible and absolutely perfect for any special occasion.

²/₃ cup unsalted butter at room temperature, plus more for the pans

2 cups cake flour

¼ teaspoon baking soda

1½ teaspoons baking powder

½ teaspoon salt

⅓ cup unsweetened cocoa powder

1½ cups sugar

2 large eggs

1 teaspoon pure vanilla extract

½ cup buttermilk

½ cup boiling water

Chocolate Buttercream Frosting (recipe follows)

Preheat the oven to 350°F. Line the bottom of two 8-inch round cake pans with parchment paper cut to fit and grease the bottom and the sides.

In a medium bowl, sift together the flour, baking soda, baking powder, salt, and cocoa powder, set aside.

In the bowl of a standing mixer fitted with the paddle attachment, cream together the butter and sugar on medium-high speed until light and fluffy, 2 to 3 minutes. Add the eggs, one at a time, beating well after each addition, then stir in the vanilla. Reduce the mixer speed to low and add the flour mixture and the buttermilk alternately in three additions, beginning and ending with the flour. Finally, add the boiling water and mix until smooth.

Pour the batter into the prepared pans and bake for 25 to 30 minutes, until a toothpick or cake tester inserted into the center comes out clean. Let cool in the pans on wire racks for 5 minutes. Invert the cakes onto the racks and remove the parchment paper, then immediately reinvert them and let cool completely.

Using a serrated knife, gently trim the tops of the cakes to make them level. Place the first cake layer on a cake plate and frost the top with about 1 cup of the chocolate buttercream frosting. Place the second cake layer on top, then frost the entire cake with the remaining frosting.

CHOCOLATE BUTTERCREAM FROSTING

Makes about 4 cups

4 ounces bittersweet chocolate, chopped into small pieces

1 cup (2 sticks) unsalted butter, at room temperature

7½ cups confectioners' sugar

6 to 8 teaspoons whole milk, plus more as needed

2 teaspoons pure vanilla extract

Place the chocolate in a heatproof bowl and set the bowl over a saucepan of simmering water, making sure the water doesn't touch the bottom of the bowl. Heat the chocolate, stirring occasionally, until melted and completely smooth. Set aside to cool.

In the bowl of a standing mixer fitted with the paddle attachment, cream together the butter and sugar until light and fluffy, 2 to 3 minutes. Add 6 to 8 teaspoons of the milk and stir to combine. Add the vanilla and the melted chocolate and mix well to combine. If necessary, add more milk as needed to achieve the desired consistency.

Classic Yellow Cake with Vanilla Buttercream Frosting

Makes one 9-inch double-layer cake

If you enjoy baking, then this cake should absolutely be included in your repertoire, as it is one you will find yourself making over and over again. This is one of my personal favorites, and I look forward to making it for my daughter's birthday every year. The whole family gets involved in the cake decorating, and we go to great lengths to make it look different each time. Once we decorated the cake with beautiful gold edible pearls in different sizes and placed long gold candles all around. The cake was glowing! I also love making candied daisies for a more simple yet elegant presentation. Feel free to be creative and make this classic yellow cake your own!

¾ cup (1½ sticks) unsalted butter, at room temperature, plus more for the pans

All-purpose flour, for the pans

3 cups cake flour

2½ teaspoons baking powder

1 teaspoon salt

1½ cups sugar

3 large eggs

1 teaspoon pure vanilla extract

1 cup whole milk

Vanilla Buttercream Frosting (recipe follows)

Preheat the oven to 350°F. Butter two 9 x 2-inch round cake pans and then dust them with all-purpose flour, tapping out any excess.

In a medium bowl, sift together the cake flour, baking powder, and salt; set aside.

In the bowl of a standing mixer fitted with the paddle attachment, cream together the butter and sugar on medium-high speed until light and fluffy, 2 to 3 minutes. Scrape down the sides of the bowl, then beat in the eggs, one at a time, until completely incorporated. Add the vanilla and mix until combined. Reduce the mixer speed to low and add the flour mixture and the milk alternately in three additions, beginning and ending with the flour. Beat until the batter is combined after each addition.

Divide the batter between the prepared pans and use a spatula or knife to smooth the tops. Bake until the cakes are light golden brown and a toothpick or cake tester inserted into the center comes out clean, 30 to 35 minutes. Let cool in the pans on wire racks for 15 to 20 minutes. Invert the cakes onto the racks, then immediately reinvert them and let cool completely.

Using a serrated knife, gently trim the tops of the cakes to make them level. Place the first cake layer on a cake plate and frost the top with about 1 cup of the vanilla buttercream frosting. Place the second layer on top, then frost the entire cake with the remaining frosting.

VANILLA BUTTERCREAM FROSTING

Makes about 4 cups

1 cup (2 sticks) unsalted butter, at room temperature

7½ cups confectioners' sugar

6 to 8 teaspoons whole milk

2 teaspoons pure vanilla extract

In the bowl of a standing mixer fitted with the paddle attachment, beat the butter on medium speed until smooth and creamy, about 2 minutes. Reduce the mixer speed to low and add the sugar and 6 teaspoons of the milk. Add the remaining 2 teaspoons milk, if necessary, to reach the desired consistency. Mix in the vanilla and beat until the buttercream is light and fluffy, 2 to 3 minutes.

Classic White Cake

Made with egg whites instead of whole eggs, the texture of this fabulous cake turns out light, fluffy, and perfectly moist. Folding the beaten egg whites into the batter instead of beating them in also leads to a softer crumb and less dense cake. I like to add Chantilly cream between the layers and top with a generous amount of cream cheese frosting, but feel free to mix it up with chocolate or vanilla frosting, if you prefer. Also, try topping this classic cake with seasonal berries, candied citrus, or chocolate shavings to make it even more unique and special.

¾ cup (1½ sticks) unsalted butter, at room temperature, plus more for the pans

2 cups all-purpose flour, plus more for the pans

1 tablespoon baking powder

⅛ teaspoon baking soda

½ teaspoon salt

1½ cups sugar

2 teaspoons pure vanilla extract

1 cup half-and-half

5 large egg whites, at room temperature

Chantilly Cream (recipe follows)

Cream Cheese Frosting (recipe follows)

Preheat the oven to 350°F. Butter two 9-inch round cake pans and then dust them with all-purpose flour, tapping out any excess; set aside.

In a medium bowl, sift together the flour, baking powder, baking soda, and salt; set aside.

In the bowl of a standing mixer fitted with the paddle attachment, cream together the butter and sugar on medium-high speed until light and fluffy, about 2 minutes. Add the vanilla and beat to combine. Reduce the mixer speed to low and add the flour mixture and the half-and-half alternately in three additions, beginning and ending with the flour. Beat until the batter is combined after each addition.

In the clean bowl of a standing mixer fitted with a clean whisk attachment, beat egg whites on medium-high speed until medium peaks form, then use a rubber spatula to fold the whites into the batter.

Divide the batter evenly between the prepared pans. Bake for about 30 minutes, or until a toothpick or cake tester inserted into the center comes out clean. Let cool in the pans on wire racks for 15 to 20 minutes. Invert the cakes onto the racks, then immediately reinvert them and let cool completely.

Using a serrated knife, gently trim the tops of the cakes to make them level. Place the first cake layer on a cake plate and top with about 1 cup of Chantilly cream. Place the second layer on top, then frost the entire cake with cream cheese frosting.

CHANTILLY CREAM

Makes about 1 ½ cups

¾ cup heavy cream

2 tablespoons confectioners' sugar

½ teaspoon pure vanilla extract

½ vanilla bean, split and seeds scraped

In a large bowl using a whisk or a hand mixer, beat the heavy cream, gradually adding the sugar, vanilla extract, and vanilla seeds, until stiff peaks form.

CREAM CHEESE FROSTING

Makes about 4 cups

1 cup (2 sticks) unsalted butter, at room temperature

2 (8-ounce) packages cream cheese, at room temperature

1¼ cups confectioners' sugar

1½ teaspoons pure vanilla extract

In the bowl of a standing mixer fitted with the paddle attachment, beat together the butter and cream cheese on medium-high speed until fluffy, about 2 minutes. Reduce the mixer speed to medium-low and add the sugar and vanilla, beating to combine.

Lemon Layer Cake with Lemon Buttercream Frosting

Makes one 8-inch triple-layer cake

I made this three-layer cake on The American Baking Competition *for my Surprise Inside Cake during Cake Week. I wanted it to be tall enough to make my design, and the result was a huge cake that was a stunning sight to behold. This layered sponge cake is light, airy, and lemony without being tart. I like to decorate the frosted top with candied lemons to highlight the citrus flavors already found in the cake. If you don't have the time to make candied lemons, freshly grated lemon zest will give added flavor and make for a beautiful presentation as well. For an easy variation, scoop the batter into a lined 12-cup muffin pan, filling the cups about three-quarters full, to make delicious lemony cupcakes—and be sure to top them with buttercream frosting.*

Nonstick cooking spray, for the pans

3 cups all-purpose flour, plus more for the pans

5 large egg yolks

2½ cups sugar

Grated zest of 2 lemons, plus 1 tablespoon

½ cup fresh lemon juice

6 tablespoons (¾ stick) unsalted butter, cut into pieces

1½ teaspoons baking powder

½ teaspoon baking soda

½ teaspoon salt

¾ cup buttermilk

1 teaspoon pure vanilla extract

5 large eggs

Lemon Buttercream Frosting (recipe follows)

Preheat the oven to 325ºF and place the rack in the center. Spray three 8-inch round cake pans with nonstick cooking spray and line the bottoms with parchment paper cut to fit. Spray the parchment, then dust the pans lightly with flour and tap out any excess. Set aside.

In a heavy saucepan, combine the egg yolks and ½ cup of the sugar and whisk vigorously for 1 minute. Add the zest of 2 lemons and ¼ cup of the lemon juice and whisk for 1 minute more. Set the pan over low heat and cook gently, stirring continuously, until slightly thickened, 10 to 15 minutes. Remove the pan from the heat and stir in the butter until it has melted completely. Set the lemon curd aside to cool.

In a medium bowl, whisk together the flour, baking powder, baking soda, and salt. In a separate bowl, whisk together the buttermilk, remaining 1 tablespoon lemon zest, remaining ¼ cup lemon juice, and the vanilla.

In the bowl of a standing mixer fitted with the whisk attachment, beat together the eggs and remaining 2 cups of the sugar on medium speed until the mixture forms ribbons when the whisk is lifted out, about 2 minutes. Reduce the mixer speed to low and add the flour mixture and the buttermilk alternately in three additions, beginning and ending with the flour. Beat until completely combined after each addition.

Divide the batter evenly between the three prepared pans. Bake for about 30 minutes, or until a toothpick or cake tester inserted into the center comes out clean. Let cool in the pans on wire racks for about 10 minutes. Invert the cakes onto the racks, then immediately reinvert them and let cool completely.

Using a serrated knife, gently trim the tops of the cakes to make them level.

Place the first cake layer on a cake plate and spoon the lemon curd over the top. Place the second cake layer on top, top-side down, then repeat with remaining lemon curd. Place third and final layer on top and frost the cake completely with the buttercream frosting.

LEMON BUTTERCREAM FROSTING

Makes about 4 cups

1 cup (2 sticks) unsalted butter, at room temperature

7½ cups confectioners' sugar

6 to 8 teaspoons whole milk, plus more as needed

2 teaspoons pure vanilla extract

1 tablespoon lemon extract

2 teaspoons lemon zest

In the bowl of a standing mixer fitted with the paddle attachment, cream together the butter and sugar on medium-high speed until light and fluffy, about 2 minutes. Add 6 to 8 teaspoons of milk and continue to beat until combined. Add more milk, 1 teaspoon at a time, if necessary to achieve the desired consistency. Stir in the vanilla, lemon extract, and zest.

Orange-Almond Dacquoise

Makes one 9-inch dacquoise

I made this as the Showstopper during Dessert Week on The American Baking Competition, *and so many people in the tent were in awe of how beautiful it looked and how good it tasted.*

This stunning dessert cake is made with crisp layers of almond meringue, filled with decadent chocolate mousse and topped with an orange buttercream frosting. These three flavors work in perfect harmony to make an incredibly delicious dessert. Piping perfect meringue discs is not that hard as long as you have stenciled circles onto parchment paper to use as a guide. This is another dessert where you can change the frostings and the fillings to make it unique and different. You can also substitute the almond flour with something such as pistachio flour, which will give it a whole new taste.

Nonstick cooking spray or vegetable oil, for the pans

1 cup superfine sugar

Pinch of salt

½ cup almond flour

6 large egg whites

½ teaspoon cream of tartar

½ teaspoon pure vanilla extract

1 teaspoon pure almond extract

Chocolate Ganache Mousse (recipe follows)

Orange Buttercream Frosting (recipe follows)

1 cup whole almonds, toasted and chopped, for garnish

1 cup (about 2 ounces) shaved semisweet chocolate, for garnish

Preheat the oven to 300ºF. Spray baking sheets with nonstick cooking spray or brush with vegetable oil. Using the bottom of a 9-inch cake pan as your guide, use a pencil to trace three 9-inch circles onto parchment paper (use two sheets of parchment, if necessary). Flip the paper and place it on the prepared baking sheets.

In a medium bowl, whisk together ⅔ cup of the sugar, the salt, and the almond flour. In the bowl of a standing mixer fitted with the whisk attachment, beat the egg whites and cream of tartar until soft peaks form, then slowly add the remaining ⅓ cup sugar and beat until stiff peaks form. Whisk in both extracts. Remove the bowl from the mixer and use a rubber spatula to gently fold in the almond flour mixture, making sure not to knock all of the air out of the meringue.

Transfer the meringue to a pastry bag fitted with a ½-inch plain tip and pipe it into ¼-inch-thick circles onto the prepared baking sheets, using the circles marked on the parchment as guides. (Alternatively, divide the meringue into three equal portions and use a rubber spatula to spread it into ¼-inch-thick circles.) Bake the meringue discs for 1 to 1½ hours, until crisp and slightly golden. Remove from oven and let cool on baking sheets.

To assemble the dacquoise, place first meringue disc on a cake stand and spread half of the chocolate ganache mousse over it, to completely cover. Top with a second meringue disc and spread the remaining mousse over it, then finally set the last meringue disc over the mousse and frost the top with orange buttercream. Garnish with chopped almonds and shaved chocolate and refrigerate for at least 3 hours, until the frosting is set.

CHOCOLATE GANACHE MOUSSE

Makes 3 cups

8 ounces semisweet chocolate, chopped

½ cup whole milk

2 cups heavy cream

½ teaspoon pure vanilla extract

Place the chocolate in a medium bowl; set aside. In a small saucepan, heat the milk over medium heat until small bubbles form around the edges. Pour the hot milk over the chocolate and stir until the chocolate has completely melted. Let cool to room temperature.

In the bowl of a standing mixer fitted with the whisk attachment, whip the cream until soft peaks form, then add the vanilla. Remove the bowl from the mixer and use a rubber spatula to gently fold in the chocolate mixture.

ORANGE BUTTERCREAM FROSTING

Makes 2 cups

½ cup (1 stick) unsalted butter, at room temperature

3¾ cups confectioners' sugar

3 to 4 teaspoons whole milk

1 teaspoon pure vanilla extract

1 teaspoon orange extract

Grated zest of 1 orange

In the bowl of a standing mixer fitted with the paddle attachment, cream together the butter and sugar on medium-high speed until light and fluffy, about 2 minutes. Add 3 teaspoons of the milk. Add the remaining teaspoon milk, if necessary, to achieve the desired consistency. Add the vanilla, orange extract, and orange zest and mix to combine.

Pound Cake

The name "pound cake" refers to the traditional recipe for this type of cake, which called for a pound of butter, a pound of sugar, a pound of flour, and a pound of eggs. Although both of my grandmothers baked this cake often and in its original form, I have made a couple of adjustments and think you will really enjoy the results. I've added ingredients such as sour cream, cream cheese, and freshly grated nutmeg to create an even more tender, moist texture and to enhance the flavor. Pound cakes are perfect for easy entertaining and can be jazzed up with toppings such as macerated fresh fruit, dollops of whipped cream, or big scoops of homemade ice cream.

Nonstick cooking spray, for the pan

3 cups all-purpose flour

½ teaspoon freshly grated nutmeg

½ teaspoon salt

2 teaspoons baking powder

1 cup (2 sticks) unsalted butter, at room temperature, plus more for the pan

1 (8-ounce) package cream cheese, at room temperature

1/3 cup sour cream

2 2/3 cups sugar

6 large eggs, at room temperature

2 teaspoons pure vanilla extract

Preheat the oven to 325°F. Coat a 10-inch tube pan with cooking spray or softened butter, then sprinkle with flour and tap out any excess to coat the entire inside of pan.

In a medium bowl, whisk together the flour, nutmeg, salt, and baking powder; set aside.

In the bowl of a standing mixer fitted with the paddle attachment, beat together the butter, cream cheese, sour cream, and sugar on medium-high speed until light and fluffy, about 2 minutes. Scrape down the sides of the bowl, then beat in the eggs, one at a time, until completely incorporated. Add the vanilla. Reduce the mixer speed to low, add the flour mixture, and mix until combined.

Pour the batter into the prepared pan and bake for about 1 hour and 20 minutes, or until a toothpick or cake tester inserted into the center comes out clean. Let the cake cool slightly in the pan on a wire rack. Invert the pan onto the rack to remove the cake, then immediately reinvert the cake and let cool completely on the rack before slicing and serving.

Strawberry Shortcakes

My favorite strawberry shortcakes are found at Gibsons Bar & Steakhouse in downtown Chicago. They are absolutely enormous and are filled with heaps of beautifully ripened and sweetened strawberries and cream. I've used their version as the inspiration to create this wonderful dessert, which is especially amazing in the warmer months when strawberries are at their peak. These shortcakes are perfect to make if you're looking for something fast, easy, and delicious.

1 large egg yolk

⅓ cup half-and-half

½ teaspoon pure vanilla extract

2 cups all-purpose flour

⅓ cup plus 3 tablespoons granulated sugar

1 tablespoon plus ¾ teaspoon baking powder

⅛ teaspoon baking soda

Pinch of salt

½ cup (1 stick) unsalted butter, cut into pieces

⅓ cup heavy cream

¼ to ⅓ cup turbinado sugar

1 pint strawberries, hulled and sliced

Chantilly Cream (page 160)

Fresh mint sprigs, for garnish

Preheat the oven to 425°F. Line a baking sheet with parchment paper.

In a small bowl, whisk together the egg yolk, half-and-half, and vanilla; set aside. In the bowl of a food processor, combine the flour, 3 tablespoons of the granulated sugar, the baking powder, baking soda, and salt and pulse to combine. Add the butter and pulse until the mixture resembles coarse crumbs. Add the egg and half-and-half mixture and pulse until a moist dough forms.

Spoon the dough in 3-inch mounds on the prepared baking sheet, spacing them at least 1 inch apart. Brush the tops with the heavy cream and sprinkle with the turbinado sugar. Alternatively, roll the dough into a ¾-inch-thick round and use a 3-inch biscuit cutter to cut out shortcakes. Place on prepared baking sheet about 1 inch apart. Gather the scraps, reroll the dough, and cut as many rounds as you can. Bake the shortcakes until golden and a toothpick or cake tester inserted into the center comes out clean, about 12 minutes. Transfer to wire racks to cool while you prepare the strawberries.

In a medium bowl, combine the strawberries with the remaining ⅓ cup granulated sugar and stir to coat. Refrigerate for about 25 minutes to macerate and bring all the juices out.

To assemble, slice the cooled shortcakes in half and set the bottom halves on a plate. Spoon a dollop of Chantilly cream on the bottom and then top with macerated strawberries. Finish by setting the shortcake top over the strawberries. Garnish with fresh mint.

Peanut-Vanilla Chiffon Roll with Peanut Praline and Gold-Dusted Peanuts

For the final Signature Bake on The American Baking Competition, *each contestant was asked to make a peanut-based dessert and make it elegant. Boy, did this really push each of us to dig deep. Peanuts and elegant just didn't seem to go hand in hand! Well, that was until I came up with this peanut-vanilla chiffon roll, a delicate cake with a delicious chocolate-peanut mousse filling coated with a semisweet chocolate ganache, then sprinkled with decadent peanut praline. Once it was finished, I was so happy about the way it turned out, I nearly started crying! It turned out to be a very beautiful and elegant cake, and the judges loved it—you could even say they were "nuts" about it. Their one suggestion was that I add more of the peanut praline throughout the cake because it was so tasty, so I have amped it up in this recipe.*

Nonstick cooking spray, for the pan

1 cup all-purpose flour

1 teaspoon baking soda

1 teaspoon baking powder

$\frac{1}{8}$ teaspoon salt

1½ cups granulated sugar

4 large egg yolks

½ cup vegetable oil

2 teaspoons pure vanilla extract and half of a vanilla bean, split and seeds scraped

½ cup water plus 1 tablespoon

6 large egg whites

Confectioners' sugar, for dusting

Chocolate-Peanut Mousse (recipe follows)

Chocolate Ganache Glaze (recipe follows)

Peanut Praline (recipe follows)

Gold-Dusted Peanuts (recipe follows)

Fresh mint sprigs, for garnish

Preheat the oven to 350°F. Line a jelly roll pan with parchment paper and spray the paper with nonstick cooking spray.

In a large bowl, sift together the flour, baking soda, baking powder, and salt, then whisk in 1 cup of the granulated sugar. In a separate bowl, whisk together the egg yolks, oil, vanilla, vanilla bean, and ½ cup water. Fold in the flour mixture and set aside.

In the bowl of a standing mixer fitted with the whisk attachment, beat together the egg whites and the remaining ½ cup granulated sugar until stiff and shiny. Gently fold the egg whites into the batter one third at a time, being careful not to knock the air out of the whites, until the batter is light and fluffy.

Pour the batter into the prepared pan, spread it evenly with offset spatula, and bake for 12 to 14 minutes or when touched it slightly bounces back. Let cool completely in the pan on a wire rack.

Dust the cooled cake with confectioners' sugar and place a sheet of parchment paper over the top. Set the bottom of a second jelly roll pan on the parchment paper, and holding both pans together, flip the cake onto the back of the second jelly roll pan. Remove the parchment paper on which the cake was baked and place a clean piece of parchment paper on top, then flip the cake back onto an inverted jelly roll pan so the cake is right-side up.

Spread the chocolate-peanut mousse over the cake, leaving a 1-inch border around the edge, and roll the cake from one short end into a log shape, using the parchment paper as a guide.

Pour the glaze over the cake, and once it has hardened, transfer the cake to a serving platter. Decorate the cake with peanut praline, gold-dusted peanuts, and mint sprigs. Refrigerate until ready to serve.

CHOCOLATE-PEANUT MOUSSE

8 ounces semisweet chocolate, chopped

½ cup whole milk

1 cup heavy cream

1 teaspoon pure vanilla extract

1 cup unsalted peanuts, finely ground

Place the chocolate in a medium bowl and set aside. In a small saucepan, heat the milk over medium heat until small bubbles start to form around the edges, then pour hot milk over the chocolate and stir until the chocolate has melted completely and the mixture is smooth. Stir in vanilla. Let cool to room temperature.

In a medium bowl using a whisk or in the bowl of a standing mixer fitted with the whisk attachment, beat the cream until soft peaks form. Gently fold the cream and ground peanuts into the cooled chocolate, cover, and refrigerate until ready to use.

CHOCOLATE GANACHE GLAZE

8 ounces semisweet chocolate, chopped

¾ cup heavy cream

2 tablespoons corn syrup

Place the chocolate in a medium bowl and set aside. In a medium saucepan, combine the cream and corn syrup and bring to a boil over medium-high heat. Pour the cream mixture over the chocolate and stir until the chocolate has completely melted and the mixture is smooth. Keep warm if not using immediately.

PEANUT PRALINE

Nonstick cooking spray for the pan

1 cup sugar

1 cup lightly salted peanuts

Lightly oil a baking sheet with nonstick cooking spray. Place the sugar in a small saucepan and heat over medium-high heat, stirring continuously with a wooden spoon, until the sugar has melted and caramelized to a medium brown color. Add the peanuts and stir to coat, cooking for about 20 seconds more. Turn the caramelized nuts onto the prepared baking sheet, spread them into an even layer, and set aside to harden. Use your hands or the back of a spoon to break the praline into pieces.

GOLD-DUSTED PEANUTS

2 cups lightly salted peanuts

1 to 1½ tablespoons canola oil

1 to 2 tablespoons edible gold dust or sprinkles

In a medium bowl, use a rubber spatula to combine the peanuts with the oil, then toss them with the gold dust.

Petit Four Flag Cake

This was the last dessert I baked on the finale of The American Baking Competition. *For the 72 Miniatures Challenge, I decided to use my pastries to re-create the aesthetic of the United States of America's flag. I wanted to use these petits fours and make a flag out of them, but I had very limited space and lots of finale nerves to deal with. Despite the challenges, with a little effort and precision I was able to create a beautiful design out of these moist little desserts. The cakes are light and airy, and are filled with raspberry whipped cream, coated with a white chocolate glaze, and then topped with fresh berries. Now, you don't have to make a flag design like I did for the show, but lined up on any dessert display these little cakes will really stand out. You can make this as a single cake as well, but if you have the time it's definitely worth making them bite-size.*

3 tablespoons unsalted butter, melted, plus more for the pan

1¼ cups cake flour, plus more for the pan

²/₃ cup sugar

¹/₈ teaspoon salt

2 large eggs

4 large egg yolks

1 teaspoon pure vanilla extract

Raspberry Whipped Cream (recipe follows)

Petit Four Glaze (recipe follows)

Mixed fresh berries, for garnish

Preheat the oven to 350ºF. Butter and flour a 9-inch square cake pan, then line the bottom with a 9-inch square of parchment paper cut to fit. Butter and flour the paper.

In a medium bowl, sift the flour with 1 tablespoon of the sugar and the salt and set aside. In the bowl of a standing mixer fitted with the whisk attachment, beat the eggs, egg yolks, and remaining sugar on medium speed until pale yellow and tripled in volume. Add the vanilla, then remove the bowl from the mixer and gently fold in the flour mixture and melted butter.

Pour the batter into the prepared cake pan and bake for 20 to 25 minutes, until a toothpick or cake tester inserted into the center comes out clean. Let cool for 5 to 10 minutes in the pan on a wire rack. Invert the cake onto the rack to remove the pan, then immediately reinvert the cake and let cool completely on the rack.

Using a 3-inch round or square cookie cutter, cut out mini cakes. Slice the cakes in half horizontally and fill with whipped cream, then replace the top. Glaze the cakes while the glaze is still warm, and decorate with your choice of berries.

RASPBERRY WHIPPED CREAM

1 cup heavy cream

2 tablespoons seedless raspberry preserves or preserves of your choice

2 teaspoons Chambord

In a large bowl using a whisk or in the bowl of a standing mixer fitted with the whisk attachment, beat together all the ingredients until stiff peaks form. Use immediately or keep refrigerated for up to 24 hours.

PETIT FOUR GLAZE

12 ounces white chocolate, chopped

$^2/_3$ cup heavy cream

Place the white chocolate in a medium bowl and set aside. In a small saucepan, heat the cream over medium-high heat until small bubbles start to form around the edges, then pour the hot cream over the chocolate and stir until the chocolate has melted completely and the mixture is smooth. Let cool slightly before pouring over the cakes while still warm.

Pastry and Pie Dough

Introduction to Pastry and Pie Dough

Puff pastry, much like croissant dough, is a labor of love. Although it takes time, your patience and work will pay off when you achieve the result: a rich, buttery, and flaky layered dough that store-bought versions simply can't replicate. It's important to allow the dough time to fully chill and rest between rolling and folding, as overworked dough will be tough and difficult to work with. Also, keep your work surface well dusted with flour, but use a pastry brush to remove excess flour from the dough between each rolling-and-folding session. Puff pastry is incredibly versatile and can be used in savory dishes, such as the Chicken Potpie (page 34), or sweet treats, like Napoleons with Chocolate Mousse (page 187). You can freeze leftover puff pastry for up to a month and thaw it when ready to use.

Pie dough, otherwise known as pâte brisée, is the building block for delicious pies and desserts. On *The American Baking Competition*, our judges were more discerning about the piecrust than any other element of the dessert and stressed that the flaky, crisp texture and buttery taste of the crust separates a good pie from a great one. Although making your own pie dough may seem intimidating, the process of bringing together the basic dough ingredients—flour, fat, and water—is actually quite easy and very fast. Add a pinch of salt, sugar, or other ingredients like chives or lemon zest to change the flavor depending on what type of pie you are making. For best results, it's very important to start with well-chilled ingredients . . . I cannot stress this enough! If you do not have a food processor handy, use a pastry cutter or two knives to cut the cold fat into the flour, making sure to leave pea-size, coarse pieces of the fat visible throughout so that they will melt into the crust when baked and make it properly flaky.

Puff Pastry

Makes about 2 pounds

4 cups all-purpose flour, plus more for dusting

1 teaspoon sea salt

1 cup ice water

2 cups (4 sticks) plus 2 tablespoons unsalted butter, cold

In the bowl of a standing mixer fitted with the dough hook, combine 2 cups of the flour and the salt. Add the cold water and knead on low speed until a smooth batter forms. Cut 2 tablespoons of the butter into pieces and scatter them on top. Raise the mixer speed to medium, then slowly add the remaining 2 cups flour and knead until a soft elastic dough forms, 3 to 5 minutes.

Turn out the dough onto a lightly floured surface and knead, adding flour as necessary, until no longer sticky, about 30 seconds. Shape the dough into a rectangle, wrap it in plastic, and refrigerate for 1 hour.

Place the remaining 1 pound cold butter between two pieces of plastic wrap or parchment paper. Use a rolling pin to beat the butter until it becomes pliable. Keep beating the butter and shape it into a 6-inch square about ½ inch thick. If the butter gets too warm, return it to the refrigerator until firm again. Wrap the butter block in plastic and refrigerate until ready to use.

Place the chilled dough on a lightly floured surface and roll it out into a 12-inch square. Unwrap the butter block and place it in the center of the dough. Fold each corner of the dough in to meet at the center, completely covering the butter block. Pat the dough with your hands to form a 6- to 8-inch square. Flip the dough over so it is seam-side down on the work surface. Roll out the dough into a rectangle about 24 inches long and 8 inches wide. Position the dough block with one short side facing you. Fold down the top third of the dough to the center, then fold the bottom third over that, as if you were folding a letter. Rotate the dough clockwise so the fold is to your left. Wrap the dough block in plastic and refrigerate for about 30 minutes.

Repeat the rolling-and-folding process for six more turns, making sure you refrigerate the dough block for 30 minutes between turns and always starting with the seam to your left. After the final turn, wrap the dough block in plastic and refrigerate for 4 hours and up to overnight before rolling and baking as directed in the recipe.

Napoleons with Chocolate Mousse

Makes 4 napoleons

In week 6 of The American Baking Competition, *I made these desserts for the Technical Bake Challenge and was super excited when I won! The victory helped me become the "Star Baker" for that week and established my standing as a true contender for the overall win. These napoleons, otherwise known as mille-feuilles, are pastries made by layering crisp, flaky puff pastry with whipped cream and chocolate mousse and topping them with a layer of vanilla glaze. Beautiful in appearance and delicious to eat, these are definitely a winner.*

All-purpose flour, for dusting

1 recipe Puff Pastry (page 185) or frozen store-bought puff pastry, such as Dufour

4 ounces semisweet chocolate, chopped

¼ cup half-and-half

2¾ cups heavy cream

¾ cup confectioners' sugar

1½ teaspoons pure vanilla extract

½ vanilla bean, split and seeds scraped

Preheat the oven to 400°F. Line two baking sheets with parchment paper.

On a lightly floured surface, roll out the puff pastry into a rectangle about 8 x 20 inches and about ⅛ inch thick, making sure you keep the lines of the dough straight. Using a ruler, cut the large rectangle into twelve 2½ x 3½-inch rectangles. Place the rectangles on the prepared baking sheets and bake for about 20 minutes. Set aside to cool while you make the filling.

Place the chocolate in a medium bowl and set aside. In a small saucepan, heat the half-and-half over medium-high heat until small bubbles start to form around the edges, then pour it over the chocolate and stir until the chocolate has completely melted. Let cool slightly.

In the bowl of a standing mixer fitted with the whisk attachment, beat 1½ cups of the heavy cream on medium speed until medium peaks form. Remove the bowl from the mixer and use a rubber spatula to gently fold in the cooled melted chocolate until incorporated. Transfer the chocolate mousse to a pastry bag fitted with a ½-inch star tip and refrigerate until ready to use.

In the clean bowl of a standing mixer fitted with the whisk attachment, beat together 1 cup of the heavy cream, ¼ cup of the confectioners' sugar, ½ teaspoon of the vanilla extract, and the vanilla bean seeds on medium-high speed until medium peaks form. Transfer the whipped cream to a pastry bag fitted with a ½-inch star tip and refrigerate until ready to use.

In a medium bowl, whisk together the remaining ¼ cup heavy cream, ½ cup confectioners' sugar, and 1 teaspoon vanilla extract until the mixture is incorporated and has thickened; set the vanilla glaze aside.

To assemble, lay a puff pastry rectangle on a clean work surface and pipe stars of the whipped cream in rows over the surface of the rectangle. Stack another rectangle on top of the whipped cream, then pipe stars of the chocolate mousse completely over the top. Using an offset spatula or knife, frost the third rectangle with the vanilla glaze, and place it glaze-side up on top of the mousse. Repeat until you have assembled all four napoleons.

Classic Pie Dough

Makes one 9-inch piecrust

1¼ cups all-purpose flour

1 teaspoon salt

½ cup (1 stick) unsalted butter, cut into pieces and kept cold

3 to 4 tablespoons ice water

In the bowl of a food processor, combine the flour, salt, and butter. Pulse until the mixture resembles coarse meal. Slowly add 3 tablespoons water and pulse until the dough just holds together when pressed between your fingers. If the dough is too dry, add more water 1 teaspoon at a time until the desired consistency is reached. Remove the dough from the bowl, form it into a disc, and wrap it in plastic. Chill the dough for about 30 minutes before using.

Pie Dough with Lemon Zest

Makes one 9-inch piecrust

1¼ cups all-purpose flour

Pinch of salt

1 teaspoon sugar

1 tablespoon grated lemon zest

½ cup (1 stick) unsalted butter, cut into pieces and kept cold

3 to 4 tablespoons ice water

In the bowl of a food processor, combine the flour, salt, sugar, zest, and butter. Pulse until the mixture resembles coarse meal. Slowly add 3 tablespoons water and pulse until the dough just holds together when pressed between your fingers. If the dough is too dry, add more water 1 teaspoon at a time until the desired consistency is reached. Remove the dough from the bowl, form it into a disc, and wrap it in plastic. Chill the dough for about 30 minutes before using.

Apple Cider–Spiked Pie Dough

Makes one 9-inch piecrust

1¼ cups all-purpose flour

Pinch of salt

½ teaspoon baking powder

1 teaspoon sugar

½ cup (1 stick) unsalted butter, cut into pieces and kept cold

3 to 4 tablespoons ice water

½ teaspoon apple cider vinegar

In the bowl of a food processor, combine the flour, salt, baking powder, sugar, and butter. Pulse until the mixture resembles coarse meal. Slowly add 3 tablespoons water and the vinegar and pulse until the dough just holds together when pressed between your fingers. If the dough is too dry, add more water 1 teaspoon at a time until the desired consistency is reached. Remove the dough from the bowl, form it into a disc, and wrap it in plastic. Chill the dough for about 30 minutes before using.

Pie Dough with Chives

Makes one 9-inch piecrust

1¼ cups all-purpose flour

Pinch of salt

½ cup (1 stick) unsalted butter, cut into pieces and kept cold

¼ cup chopped fresh chives

3 to 4 tablespoons ice water

In the bowl of a food processor, combine the flour, salt, and butter. Pulse until the mixture resembles coarse meal. Add the chives and pulse to combine. Slowly add 3 tablespoons water and pulse until the dough just holds together when pressed between your fingers. If the dough is too dry, add more water 1 teaspoon at a time until the desired consistency is reached. Remove the dough from the bowl, form it into a disc, and wrap it in plastic. Chill the dough for about 30 minutes before using.

Tart Dough

Makes enough for twelve 3-inch tartlets or one 9-inch tart

1¼ cups all-purpose flour

¼ cup sugar

Pinch of salt

½ cup (1 stick) unsalted butter, cut into pieces and kept cold

1 large egg yolk

1 teaspoon pure vanilla extract

3 to 4 tablespoons ice water

In the bowl of a food processor, combine the flour, sugar, and salt. Pulse to combine, then add the butter and pulse until the mixture resembles coarse meal. Add the egg yolk, vanilla, and 3 tablespoons ice water and pulse until the dough forms a ball. If the dough is too dry, add more water 1 teaspoon at a time until the desired consistency is reached. Remove the dough from the bowl, form it into a disc, and wrap it in plastic. Chill the dough for about 30 minutes before using.

Gougères

Light, airy, and addicting, these classic savory French cheese puffs are great to serve when you are entertaining. I made these for a French-themed dinner party and everyone was absolutely raving about them! For me, these are the perfect hors d'oeuvres because in addition to being delicious, they are easy to make and they are always a huge hit. You can even bake them ahead of time and freeze them in an airtight container for up to two months. Just wrap them in foil and bake at 350ºF for about 15 minutes to reheat before serving.

½ cup half-and-half

½ cup (1 stick) unsalted butter

½ teaspoon salt

Pinch of cayenne pepper

1 cup all-purpose flour

4 large eggs, plus 1 for egg wash

1½ cups grated fontina cheese

2 tablespoons grated Pecorino Romano cheese

¼ teaspoon fresh ground black pepper

1 teaspoon grainy brown mustard

Preheat the oven to 425ºF. Line two baking sheets with parchment paper.

In a medium saucepan, bring the half-and-half, butter, salt, and cayenne to a boil over medium-high heat. Add the flour all at once and beat vigorously with a wooden spoon until the dough starts to come together and pulls away from the sides of the pan, 3 to 5 minutes.

Remove the pan from the heat and let stand for a few minutes to cool slightly. Using a wooden spoon, vigorously beat in 4 eggs one at a time, beating fast so the eggs do not have time to scramble. Stir in 1½ cups of the fontina, the pecorino, black pepper, and mustard until the dough is smooth.

Prepare egg wash; in a small bowl beat one egg with ¼ cup water with a fork until well blended and set aside.

Drop rounded tablespoons of the dough on the prepared baking sheets, leaving 2 inches between each. Brush them with egg wash and sprinkle evenly with the remaining ½ cup fontina. Bake the gougères for 20 to 25 minutes, rotating the pans halfway through the baking time, until puffed and golden. Let cool on the baking sheets for 5 minutes before serving.

Soufflés and Custards

Introduction to Soufflés and Custards

There are few dishes as impressive as perfectly puffed, light, and airy soufflés. Straight from the oven and onto the table, whether sweet or savory, they are always and without a doubt a showstopper. The trick to the perfect soufflé is to make sure the egg whites are first whipped into stiff peaks, and then gently folded into the base, making sure not to overmix, which will deflate the batter. Another great trick to giving your soufflés optimal height is to add a soufflé collar, which is simply parchment paper tied with kitchen string around the outside of the ramekin. Make sure you cut the paper so it overlaps a little where the ends meet and stands 2 to 3 inches above the top edge of the ramekin. The final presentation is sure to be so dramatic that you will bask in the glory of success and the sounds of cheers and applause filling the room. Just be sure to serve them straight out of the oven (with the parchment collars removed), as soufflés will fall after time!

I've included some of my all-time favorite recipes in this chapter, such as smooth and delicious Chocolate-Raspberry Pots de Crème (page 203), Pumpkin Custard (page 209), and a breakfast and brunch favorite, Mile-High Quiche (page 207). I also have become a bit famous for my Sunday Brunch Strata (page 211), with its layers of toasty bread, sausage, bacon, cheese, and mushrooms. I made this at a family reunion and everyone was going crazy for more—they loved it! I promised to pass along the recipe, so I'm happy to share it now.

Although making custard is a fairly straightforward process, it can be a little tricky, and an overcooked base can become lumpy and grainy. To avoid this, I usually heat the custard base in a double boiler or slowly in a saucepan, and I use an instant-read thermometer to monitor the temperature, which should never exceed 170ºF. I also cook some custards in the oven in a water bath or bain-marie, which helps prevent overcooking and curdling.

Sky-High Cheese and Chive Soufflés

Trust me when I say that you are sure to impress with the "sky-high" height, airy texture, and delectable taste of these cheesy soufflés! The addition of fresh chives adds a great fresh flavor, and the subtle hints of white pepper and nutmeg give them an earthy and warm taste. This recipe can also be used to make a 1½-quart soufflé—just add 8 to 10 minutes to the baking time.

2 to 3 tablespoons unsalted butter, at room temperature

⅓ cup finely grated Pecorino Romano cheese

5 large eggs, at room temperature, separated

6 ounces sharp white cheddar cheese, grated

⅓ cup chopped fresh chives

½ teaspoon salt

½ teaspoon freshly ground white pepper

¼ teaspoon freshly grated nutmeg

Pinch of cayenne pepper

¼ teaspoon cream of tartar

Preheat the oven to 425°F. Brush the bottom and sides of six 8-ounce ramekins with butter and sprinkle with the pecorino. Fit the ramekins with soufflé collars (see page 199) and place them on a rimmed baking pan.

In a large bowl or in the bowl of a standing mixer fitted with the whisk attachment, whisk the egg yolks until pale and thick. Stir in cheddar, chives, salt, white pepper, nutmeg, and cayenne and set aside.

In the clean bowl of a standing mixer fitted with a clean whisk attachment, whisk the egg whites and cream of tartar until stiff, glossy peaks form. Remove the bowl from the mixer and use a rubber spatula to gently fold the egg whites in four additions into the yolk mixture until incorporated, with a few streaks remaining. Be sure not to overwork the batter, which will deflate the egg whites.

Spoon the batter into the prepared ramekins until level with the top of the dishes. Bake the soufflés until set and puffed with a slight jiggle in the center, 15 to 20 minutes. Remove the parchment collars and serve immediately.

Chocolate-Raspberry Pots de Crème

Smooth, rich, and so chocolaty good, pots de crème are basically fancy chocolate puddings . . . and who doesn't adore chocolate pudding? I've added a bit of a black raspberry liqueur called Chambord to this recipe to give the dessert even more flavor and depth. I love serving make-ahead desserts like these because there is no fuss when you are entertaining—just serve them straight from the fridge and garnish with a dollop of whipped or Chantilly cream, chocolate shavings, and fresh raspberries for added elegance.

4 ounces bittersweet chocolate, chopped into small pieces

1 cup heavy cream

½ cup whole milk

¼ cup sugar

¼ teaspoon pure vanilla extract

4 large egg yolks

¼ teaspoon salt

1 tablespoon Chambord

Preheat the oven to 350°F.

Place chocolate in a medium bowl and set aside. In a small saucepan, combine the cream and milk and heat over medium heat until small bubbles start to form around the edges. Pour the hot cream mixture over the chocolate and stir until the chocolate has melted completely.

In a separate bowl, whisk together the sugar, vanilla, salt, and egg yolks until pale yellow. Slowly whisk in the melted chocolate and the Chambord. Divide the mixture evenly among six 6-ounce ramekins or pots-de-crème pots. Place the ramekins in a baking dish or pan and pour hot water into the pan until it comes halfway up the sides of the ramekins. Bake until the pots de crème are set, about 35 minutes. Remove the ramekins from the baking dish and serve the pots de crème warm, or refrigerate and serve chilled.

Chocolate-Raspberry Soufflés

Makes 6

I love pairing chocolate and raspberries together, and this soufflé is no exception! The light airy texture, offset by the rich chocolate and complexity of the raspberry liqueur, makes these soufflés irresistible. Put a dollop of fresh whipped cream on top with some fresh berries right before serving and watch your dinner guests swoon.

3 to 4 tablespoons unsalted butter, at room temperature

¾ cup granulated sugar, plus more for dusting the ramekins

8 ounces bittersweet chocolate, chopped

6 large eggs, separated

1 teaspoon pure vanilla extract

¼ teaspoon salt

½ teaspoon cream of tartar

1 teaspoon Chambord

Confectioners' sugar, for dusting

Preheat the oven to 400°F and place the rack in the center. Brush six 8-ounce ramekins with butter and coat the bottoms and sides completely with granulated sugar. Place in a baking dish or roasting pan that fits all the ramekins.

Place the chocolate in the top of a double boiler set over barely simmering water. Stir until the chocolate has melted, then remove from the heat and set aside to cool slightly.

In a medium bowl, whisk the egg yolks until pale in color, then whisk in ½ cup of the granulated sugar and the vanilla. Fold in the melted chocolate and set aside.

In the bowl of a standing mixer fitted with the whisk attachment, beat together the egg whites, salt, and cream of tartar on medium-high speed until soft peaks form. Slowly add the remaining ¼ cup granulated sugar and continue to beat until the egg whites are stiff and glossy but not dry.

Remove the bowl from the mixer and use a rubber spatula to gently fold the egg whites into the chocolate mixture until just combined, making sure not to overmix or deflate the egg whites. Spoon the mixture into the prepared ramekins, then use the back of a wooden spoon or your finger and gently go around to make a small groove between the batter and the top edge of the ramekins. This will make for a nice "hat" on the soufflé as it rises.

Transfer the ramekins to a baking dish or roasting pan and fill the dish with hot water to ½ way up the sides of the ramekins. Transfer to the oven and bake the soufflés until puffed and still slightly jiggly, 25 to 30 minutes. Gently remove ramekins from water bath.

To serve, make a well in the center of each soufflé and pour in about 1 teaspoon of Chambord, then dust with confectioners' sugar.

Mile-High Quiche

Serves 6 to 8

My favorite restaurant in Chicago, Ralph Lauren Grill, offers a spectacular quiche similar to this one on their brunch menu. My favorite host of all time, Flavia, is there to greet me at the door and assures me that this favorite quiche is ready and on hand for this spectacular brunch for me and my family. When it comes to the table, it's so high and stately that it really brings the "wow" factor. I'm all about accentuating the presentation and taste of my favorite recipes, so I decided to create my own version of this "mile-high" quiche with caramelized onions and leeks, ham, and sharp cheddar cheese. The best part is watching the reactions when I bring it to the table straight out of the oven while it's puffed, golden, and still at full height. WOW!

All-purpose flour, for dusting

1 recipe Classic Pie Dough (page 189)

2 tablespoons unsalted butter

⅓ cup extra-virgin olive oil

1 large Vidalia onion, halved and cut into ¼-inch-thick slices

1 large leek, white part only, cut into ¼-inch rings and rinsed well

¼ cup sugar

1 teaspoon minced garlic

8 large eggs

1 quart half-and-half

½ teaspoon freshly grated nutmeg

Kosher salt and freshly ground black pepper

1½ cups cubed ham

8 ounces sharp cheddar cheese, shredded

Crème fraîche, for serving

Preheat the oven to 375°F.

On a lightly floured surface, roll out the dough into a circle about 14 inches in diameter and about ¼ inch thick. Press the dough firmly into the bottom and up the sides of a 9-inch springform pan, and trim any extra dough from the top. Use your fingers to crimp around the edges, then refrigerate the dough in the pan for at least 30 minutes while you make the filling.

In a medium skillet, heat butter and oil over medium heat. Add the onions and leeks and cook, stirring occasionally, for about 5 minutes, then sprinkle with the sugar. Continue cooking the onions and leeks until they caramelize, 10 to 15 minutes, then add the garlic and cook for about 2 minutes more. When vegetables are golden brown, stir in ¼ cup water, remove from the heat, and set aside to cool.

In a large bowl, whisk together the eggs, half-and-half, nutmeg, and salt and pepper to taste. Stir in the cooled caramelized onion and leek mixture to combine.

Spread the ham and shredded cheese over the bottom of the chilled crust, then pour the egg mixture over top. Cover with aluminum foil and bake for about 1 hour and 25 minutes. Remove the foil and bake for 15 minutes more, until brown and puffy. Let cool for about 30 minutes, then remove the outer ring from the springform pan. Transfer the quiche to a serving plate and cut into wedges. Serve with a dollop of crème fraîche.

Pumpkin Custard

With such a simple preparation and outstanding result, these pumpkin custards are definitely one of my favorite go-to desserts during the holidays. It's like eating the pumpkin pie filling without the crust! Warm spices such as cinnamon and nutmeg perfectly complement the smooth, sweet pumpkin custard, and the orange zest adds a burst of brightness to the flavor. Serve warm or chilled and top with fresh whipped cream and a sprig of mint for a simple yet beautiful presentation.

2 to 3 tablespoons unsalted butter, at room temperature

Granulated sugar, for dusting

2 large eggs

½ cup packed light brown sugar

1 cup canned pure pumpkin puree

½ teaspoon freshly grated nutmeg

½ teaspoon ground cinnamon

½ teaspoon salt

1 cup heavy cream

½ teaspoon grated orange zest

Whipped Cream (page 15), for topping

Fresh mint sprigs, for garnish

Preheat the oven to 325ºF. Brush four 6-ounce ramekins with butter and coat the bottoms and sides completely with granulated sugar.

In a medium bowl, use a hand mixer to beat the eggs until frothy. Add the brown sugar, pumpkin, nutmeg, cinnamon, and salt and beat until completely blended. Stir in the heavy cream and orange zest to combine, then divide the mixture equally among the prepared ramekins.

Place the ramekins in a baking pan, then fill the pan with hot water until it comes halfway up the sides of the ramekins. Bake until the custards are set but still have a slight jiggle in the center, about 40 minutes. Serve with fresh whipped cream and garnish with mint sprigs.

Sunday Brunch Strata

This is by far one of the favorites with my family and friends, but not just for brunch! It's a hit for tailgating, Bunco night, bowling leagues, housewarming parties, baby showers . . . you are sure to be the MVP at any event if you show up with this amazing casserole. It's great because you can assemble all the ingredients the day before, refrigerate, and then bake fresh in the morning. It's also easy to change up the ingredients, use different cheeses, substitute the meats with seasonal vegetables such as broccoli, asparagus, or spinach, or add fresh herbs such as chopped parsley or basil as garnish for a beautiful presentation.

½ cup (1 stick) unsalted butter, plus more for the dish

2 pounds pork sausage meat

6 slices bacon

4 cups cubed day-old bread (about 1-inch cubes)

¾ teaspoon paprika

¾ teaspoon garlic salt

¾ teaspoon celery salt

¾ teaspoon dry sweet basil

¼ cup grated Parmesan cheese

6 large eggs

Hot sauce (optional)

2½ cups whole milk

1 (15-ounce) can cream of mushroom soup

¾ teaspoon dry mustard

1 (12-ounce) can mushrooms

3 cups shredded Colby Jack cheese

Preheat the oven to 400ºF. Butter a 9 x 13-inch glass baking dish.

In a medium skillet, brown the sausage over medium heat, using a wooden spoon to break it up as it cooks. Remove from heat, drain any excess fat from the pan, and set aside.

In a medium skillet, cook the bacon over medium heat until crisp. Reserving the bacon drippings in the pan, transfer the bacon to a paper towel–lined plate to drain, then chop it and set aside. Return the pan with the bacon drippings to medium heat and add the butter to melt it.

Place the cubed bread in a medium bowl and pour the melted butter and bacon drippings over the top. Add the paprika, garlic salt, celery salt, and sweet basil and stir to combine. Spread the bread in an even layer on a baking sheet and bake, tossing occasionally, until the cubes are browned, 10 to 15 minutes. Remove from the oven (turning the oven off) and sprinkle with the Parmesan. Set aside.

In a large bowl, whisk together the eggs, hot sauce to taste, milk, mushroom soup, and dry mustard. Fold in the cooked sausage, chopped cooked bacon, mushrooms, and Jack cheese. Spread the toasted bread cubes in the prepared baking dish and top with the egg mixture. Cover and refrigerate for 4 hours, or up to overnight.

When ready to bake, preheat the oven to 350ºF. Bake the strata until puffed and golden, 1 hour to 1 hour and 15 minutes. Let cool for 5 minutes before serving.

Index